DIVORCING, BELIEVING, BELONGING

DIVORCING, BELIEVING, BELONGING

James J. Young, C.S.P.

Paulist Press ◆ *New York/Ramsey*

Poem by Robert W. Castle from *Prayers from the Burned-Out City*, copyright 1968 by Sheed & Ward, Inc., is reprinted by permission of Andrews & Mc-Meel, Inc.

Note: This book describes many real experiences involving real people. The names and the events have been altered to protect their privacy. In a few cases where persons might be recognized, their permission has been obtained.

Library of Congress
Catalog Card Number: 84-80359

ISBN: 0-8091-2634-6

Published by Paulist Press
545 Island Road, Ramsey, N.J. 07446

Printed and bound in the
United States of America

Contents

ACKNOWLEDGEMENTS

I am grateful to friends who read the first draft of this book and made many helpful suggestions. Patricia Livingston improved the text greatly by her many sensitive comments; also LaSalle Caron, Sally DuBose, Kathy Kircher, Liz Barca, Eileen McGuire, Jack Finnegan, and Terry Ryan.

I am grateful to my sister, Ellen, and her husband, Jim, whose hospitality at their Florida home gave me the necessary undistracted space to write the book; and warm thanks to Margaret Kezer, my most generous and supportive secretary, who corrected and typed the manuscript.

To my mother and father, who taught me about permanence;
to my mentors, Jack Finnegan and Jack Egan, who taught me about compassion;
and to my divorced friends, who helped me put the two together

Introduction

As the evening wore on the stories came more slowly but more poignantly. The divorced men and women reached out to touch and hold each other as tears began to flow, at first self-consciously, then more freely. The young men and women studying for ministry sat in respectful attention, not always looking at the one sharing, sometimes playing with a shoelace, but taking in every word. It was one of those precious times when people were in deep communion.

I was the director of ministerial studies at Weston School of Theology at that time and had brought some thirty-five seminarians together for a weekend workshop on marriage ministry. As part of the workshop, I invited some of my divorced friends from the Paulist Center in Boston to share with the students what they were looking for from Church ministers. About two dozen divorced people sat with about three dozen men and women students. The conversation began in the early evening with some concrete encouragement from the divorced people about how Church ministers could be effective. As the evening wore on and the participants all felt more at ease, the divorced risked sharing their personal histories.

The next morning over breakfast a young Jesuit told me how deeply impressed he was by the divorced people he had met the night before. "I expected them to be fairly challenging and demanding about their need for ministry in the Church. I expected also that they would have some practical hints about how we might help. But what really surprised me was how much they cared about us. They weren't guilt-tripping us or beating us over the head with their own tales of mistreatment in the Church. They genuinely wanted us to be good priests and lay ministers. I never felt so supported and affirmed."

My favorite character in the Easter story is St. Thomas. It's been suggested that he's received a bad rap in Christian history. We always refer to him as "Doubting Thomas," and to this day it's a real put-down to call someone a "Doubting Thomas." I like to insist that we owe St. Thomas a great debt; because of him, we know that when Christ rose, he rose with his wounds.

We all recall how on that first Easter Sunday evening, the disciples of Jesus were all huddled fearfully behind the locked doors of the upper room. Jesus came and stood in their midst, but Thomas was absent. When the disciples later told Thomas that they had seen the Lord, he refused to believe them. In Thomas' defense, it is known that the Jews were great believers in ghosts, and Thomas may well have thought that his friends had seen the ghost of Jesus. So he insisted that he would not believe them unless he could see the Lord in the flesh and put his hands in the nailprints and in the wound in his side. A week later, they were all gathered again in the upper room, and this time Thomas was with them. The Lord appeared again, and said to Thomas, "Come here, Thomas. Put your finger into the nailprints and your hand into my side. Stop being an unbeliever, but begin to believe." Thomas knelt, touched the Lord's wounds, and exclaimed, "My Lord and my God!"

The wounds of Jesus which had been on Good Friday the badge of shame and defeat became on Easter Sunday after his resurrection an emblem of victory. With a mighty roar the stone at the entrance of the tomb was rolled back, and the risen Lord stood there in his glory. As the first streaks of dawn's early light touched his body, his wounds began to shine. His resurrection did not erase his wounds; rather it transformed them. Jesus

Christ invites us, his followers, to walk the same path he walked—a path of rejection, suffering and death. He promises us that if we too believe in a loving Father and remain faithful to him whatever befalls us, wounded as we are, we will be raised to new life like Jesus, and our wounds will shine.

My divorced friends from the Paulist Center had learned that lesson. They were not self-pitying and self-absorbed in their pain; rather their pain had been transformed into the source of new life for these seminarians. As my young Jesuit friend noted so insightfully over breakfast, their main concern was that their experience would benefit these young men and women just entering the Church's ministry, and that their hard-learned lessons bring compassion and understanding to others still hurting.

This book is a collection of insights that I've gained ministering to divorced Catholics these past ten years. They have taught me much, and through the lens of their experience they have helped me gain fresh insight into some of the most fundamental truths of our Christian faith. I have seen pain, healing, and new life over and over again. I have seen the Lord reaching out and touching his people. The design of the book and the succession of essays or meditations attempt to follow the process of the divorcing person through the trauma of broken marriage, onto the struggle to believe again and find a new sense of belonging in the Catholic community. I pray that what follows will draw others into that life-giving experience and enable them to transform their own painful experiences from badges of shame into emblems of victory.

Divorcing

Leaving

I'll never forget Molly. Your heart would have gone out to her when she came to her first support group meeting. Her husband had left a week before with another woman. Molly came home from a double shift at the hospital to find a note from him saying it was all over. Molly shared how she had given her all to the marriage; there had been difficult problems, but she was willing to continue in counseling. She was determined not to give up on the relationship. She had not expected marriage to be a bed of roses, and she knew there would be some problems. But her husband made the fatal decision. At that first meeting the pain was etched on Molly's face.

Sometimes we assume that the person who leaves, such as Molly's husband, has it the easiest; he takes off and leaves his problems behind. The Mollies, who are left behind, seem to suffer worse in the process. Many observers, however, suggest that both hurt badly, but somewhat differently. The one left behind does struggle with feelings of worthlessness and rejection; she now has to deal with a tangle of problems she didn't want. Yet the one who makes the decision to end the marriage is often tormented with guilt, regret and fear. He's the home-wrecker, the cruel brute, a person lacking in feeling and commitment.

There was a time in American society when the vast majority of divorces were initiated by men, but over the last twenty years women have begun to take more initiative in ending intolerable marriages. By 1975 half of the divorce actions in the

United States were being introduced by women. (Court actions
are not always an accurate indicator of who actually took the initiative in terminating the relationship, since lawyers often suggest that one or the other file for various legal reasons.)
Changing role concepts in marriage, altered religious, social and
cultural attitudes, and financial independence increasingly have
put men and women on an equal footing when it comes to re-
solving a bad marriage.

At one time we seemed to get more "victims" at our support
group meeting. It's likely that those who felt innocent in the
breakup of the marriage felt more comfortable about coming to a
Church group for sympathy.` This seemed especially true of
many of the men who came. In recent years, we are meeting
more men and women at our meetings who took the initiative in
divorcing; many insist that they did so only after lengthy consultation with counselors, friends and priests; some will even defend the decision as an act of Christian courage. Many women
will say that they never thought they would have the heart to do
it, but finally felt there was no alternative. Men will say that
they knew their action would cause unbelievable stress for their
wives, but they hoped that they would both come out on the
other side of divorce, better off than they were.

Leaving is terribly difficult for Catholics because we have
all been raised to believe that marriage is always "for better, for
worse; for richer, for poorer; in sickness and in health." "When
does the balance tip," Molly asked me—"when the continuation
of the marriage can no longer be justified?" My response to such
a question is always that the Church calls partners to marital fidelity. Christian experience teaches that one can grow as a human person and as a Christian by persevering in a flawed
relationship. God's grace is always there for those who struggle
in marriage. We know that there are many marriages which
would never get a ten out of ten rating, but which nonetheless
bring security, happiness and Christian well-being to many peo-

ple. When is a marriage judged destructive? When do things get
so bad that the continuing effects are overwhelmingly negative
for all involved, and separation alone would hold out the hope of
finding some peace? Such delicate decisions require much counsel and prayerful discernment, and there are certainly cases
where all agree there is no other alternative. Unfortunately,
given the emotionally-charged atmosphere of many troubled relationships, such decisions are often made amid great stress and
under great pressure.

I've met men and women who made the decision to divorce
with great reluctance and after much soul-searching; they soon
knew that they had done the right thing because the gain for all
was so obvious. I've met other men and women who believe that
they made a mistake and acted precipitously in ending a marriage; they know now that they acted impulsively, rashly and
without appropriate consultation; maybe they waited too long to
get help, but whatever, they did it, and once done, there was no
way to get the shattered pieces of the relationship back together
again. In walking out, they set into motion a process of alienation which could not be reversed, a breach which could not be
healed. I've met many people who confess openly that the
breakup of the marriage was their fault. Drinking, workahol-
ism, neglect, infidelity—these things were rationalized until the
very foundation of the marriage had been eroded.

In this ministry, the Church greets leavor or leavee, right
one or wrong one, innocent one or guilty one, with the mercy of
Christ. We don't encourage rehearsing injuries, continually laying blame or wallowing in the role of victim. We don't recommend beating oneself endlessly over the head when one has been
at fault. (There may be a time in counseling or spiritual direction when such learning about one's action and motives may not
only be necessary but helpful.) This ministry calls men and
women, once the marriage is over and truly beyond resuscita-
tion, to pray for healing and reconciliation.

There have been many cases where recently separated persons came to divorce meetings, got a realistic view of what divorce means from those present, and were motivated to try again at saving the marriage. I have seen many such couples negotiate not only a reunion but a better marriage. But where there is no hope of getting back together again, reconciliation with God and all those involved in the failed marriage is still necessary. One should seek peace with God, praying for God's mercy and asking God's forgiveness for any wrong that one may have done in the process of the marriage breakup. Reconciliation with one's former spouse can mean that acceptance, forbearance and forgiveness replace rancor and recrimination in the post-divorce relationship. Molly later told me that after many painful months, she finally had been able to sit down with her husband and begin to talk. She invited him to work at a truce, some way of getting along, especially for the sake of their children who were very upset. He broke down and said he would try.

Again and again at meetings I've heard people encourage others to call off the warfare and begin to work at a peaceful, new relationship for the sake of everyone involved. There can be no healing and reconciliation when all of one's energies are involved in getting back at each other. Whether leavor or leavee, one has to free up one's energies from the past and begin to invest them in the present and the future. Group members wisely avoid negative judgments of one another, preferring not to affix innocence or guilt, but rather to call those present to reconciliation and healing.

I remember Greg, a middle-aged military officer, who told me that the breakup of his marriage was truly his fault. He had become caught up in "life in the fast lane," and "outgrew" his wife of fifteen years. He thought she would go to pieces when he left, but she surprised him. She was shocked and devastated at first, but then pulled herself together; she proved something to him about the resourcefulness of career-military wives. He was already involved in a new relationship which he hoped would lead to marriage, but the woman stopped seeing him after several months. He was wrecked now, but was unable to reach out to anyone for help. He was torn with guilt, and felt there was no one he could turn to; his kids avoided him. He came to the base chapel one Saturday afternoon, and without much preparation went to confession to a priest he had never met. He poured it all out in the face-to-face encounter with the priest. The priest listened, read the Scripture passage about the prodigal son, prayed with him, gave him absolution, and embraced him with the greeting of peace at the end. Greg was overwhelmed; he had expected to have the riot act read to him, not to find understanding and forgiveness. The priest ended with the words of Jesus: "Neither will I condemn you; go your way and sin no more!" That was the turning point for Greg, and from that moment on he began to get his life together.

Is it better to stay or leave? Our Christian instinct is always to say it is better to stay. It is better to rely on God's help to work through problems and conflicts and grow together as husband and wife in the process. The Church will always insist that true love is tested and proven in adversity and suffering. Yet there are times when divorce may be the only Christian solution available to an intolerable, destructive relationship. In divorce ministry we try to minister to those who must make such frightening decisions. We try to be present also to those who have such decisions visited upon them. To all these men and women, Mollies and Gregs, guilty or innocent, right or wrong, the Church community offers the healing, reconciling love of Christ. Divorce may be the end of a marriage relationship but it is not the end of life. The Lord invites all to leave the sadness behind and to begin to live again.

Rejection

"*G*etting married was the most important decision I ever made in my life," Tim told me. "I thought I gave myself, heart and soul, to my wife. I assumed we'd live happily ever after. I really liked being married. When my wife said she didn't love me, and didn't want to be married anymore, I couldn't believe it. After a while I told myself I could handle it, and that I'd get over it. But I never expected to hurt so bad so long. Down deep, I think the rejection hurt the most—I'll never forget that night she told me she didn't love me."

If love is the most powerful positive emotion, rejection may well be the most powerful negative emotion. Just as love builds one up, draws out the best in oneself, makes one feel on top of the world, rejection makes one question one's worth, knocks the bottom out of one's self-image and pushes one to the depths of doubt and despair. Rejection is a wounding that takes a long time to heal; overcoming that sense of worthlessness and betrayal takes many months, sometimes many years. Getting over it is a long, slow process of regaining a sense of one's personal value and experiencing oneself in new, affirming ways. Recovery requires learning to love oneself all over again in some very new ways, and risking to love others again.

"I guess I should have seen it coming," Laurie said. "Gone were all the little things that husbands and wives do for one another that make a marriage beautiful. He had been telling me he didn't love me in so many subtle ways for so long, but I blocked all the messages. I guess I just couldn't face the fact that he didn't love me. And when the final confrontation came, I couldn't accept it; I kept trying to tell myself he didn't mean it. Even after he left, I kept telling myself he would come back. I couldn't deal with the rejection!"

Marriage is the most significant decision most people make in their lives. When one chooses a marriage partner, one chooses a companion for life—someone he can count on, someone he can trust, someone who will care for him no matter what, someone he can love and give himself to and someone he can make happy. Even though we've lived with a lot of divorce in American society for the past twenty years, and even though most people have known someone close to them who has gotten divorced, getting divorced has not gotten any easier. Someone once suggested that getting divorced is like being in an auto accident; if we studied the national statistics and thought of all the potential danger involved, we would all drive much more carefully. We always think that auto accidents happen to other people, never to us. Part of the shock of divorce is that this was never supposed to happen. "My marriage not work? Me, rejected? Never!" Tim said.

Furthermore, even though we've lived with so much divorce over the last generation, the American desire to have marriages that last for life has not been diminished. In 1970, NBC and the Associated Press conducted a national survey on attitudes about marriage. The researchers found that fully 90% of Americans felt that it was most desirable to have one happy marriage that lasted until death. Ten years later, in 1980, they reduplicated the survey, and found that the 90% still held firm. Americans continued to want happy marriages that lasted until death. In the ten year interval, something had changed; a much greater acceptance of divorce, as the ordinary solution to an intolerable marriage, had taken hold. By 1980 over 70% now believed that if a marriage for life didn't work, the partners should have the freedom to divorce and marry again, if they chose.

This deep-seated human desire to have a marriage for life seems to further deepen the pain of rejection. "How could this have happened to me? What did I do wrong? What's going to become of the rest of my life? There's nobody else I want to be married to," Tim said. It is sometimes said that the worst put-downs we can lay on people in our society is to call them "losers" or "rejects." Such labels imply worthlessness, uselessness, even fault. "Am I just someone who doesn't have it? Did I deceive myself all these years thinking I was reasonably attractive and reasonably competent and a reasonably decent person, only to find out the truth now—I'm really a broken wing, a wipe-out," Laurie sobbed.

Those feelings can stew over time in one's consciousness and produce behaviors which personify the negative self-appraisal. Divorcing people can get into a lot of personal trouble—make rash decisions about finances and family obligations, stay away from friends and possible sources of help, getting involved in new relationships for which they're not emotionally ready. Some may even unconsciously set up new rejections as a way of further punishing themselves. They can further alienate family and friends, and resist ordinary overtures for assistance. One woman told me that her sense of rejection was so keen that she went into a two-year "blue funk": "I just pulled back, withdrew, did only the bare survival things, and some of them I didn't do too well. It took me a while to understand that the rejection I experienced was by one very complex person, my former husband, for very complicated personal reasons. I began to see that his choosing not to love me did not mean I could not be loved by someone else. Someone else might well see what he could not see."

For most people the pain of rejection begins to ease with the passage of time, when the wounds begin to heal. There is a survival instinct in most people that gradually begins to kick into gear—opening one up to new friends, new experiences, and one's new life opportunities. However, the wound of rejection never completely seems to disappear, leaving always some sensitive scar tissue. (Some people may need professional counseling to help with a persistent low self-image when it cripples them over a very long period of time.)

For prayerful Christians, a reflection on the rejection which Jesus experienced himself can be a source of spiritual energy and spiritual healing at this time. Here was a man who was truly innocent—not just innocent in the sense that he had never done wrong, but innocent in that all his relationships were caring and loving.

In that familiar story in the Gospel of John (8:1–8) where the woman caught in adultery is brought to Jesus, we remember how he said to her accusers, "Let him who is without sin among you cast the first stone." One by one they slipped away, and he was left alone with the woman. Imagine the look in his face when he said to her, "Where are all those who have condemned you? . . . Neither will I condemn you; go your way and sin no more." I like to dwell on that encounter and think of the love and acceptance that must have been in Jesus' eyes when he spoke with the trembling woman. Many of the men who had looked at her before had done so with lust and hatred. Here was a man who looked at her with innocence, not gazing at her as someone to be used, but rather embracing her as a sister to be cherished. This encounter, in which she experienced the healing love of God, made it possible for her not to sin anymore.

Jesus was innocent, and gave himself without guardedness to those in need; he was an obedient servant of his Father and a faithful friend; he brought light and peace into a dark, suffering world. Yet he was betrayed and handed over to be executed like a common criminal. Imagine the heartbreak and the devastation that he who was so innocent experienced when his people rejected him: "Give us Barabbas!" Imagine the pain when his friends abandoned him: "Before the cock crows, you will deny me three times!" So deep was his sense of loss and pain that from the cross, he cried out, "My God, my God! Why have you abandoned me?"

It is strengthening to know that we have a brother in Jesus Christ who has known rejection, even deeper than anything we could experience. How close he is to those who experience rejection in this life! He who experienced rejection is embraced in love by his Father and raised to new life, and so he embraces us with love and offers us new life and the courage to love. In all his appearances after his resurrection, he reaches out to those who had rejected him and offers them peace.

Rejection is never welcome; it is not something we would ever want to do to anyone else. Yet for the believing person, the experience of rejection can be the pathway not only to deeper self-acceptance but to deeper acceptance of others. The Lord calls the rejected to choose life again and risk loving again. The trauma of rejection can make us ever more alert to the many small rejections which wound so many people and elicit from us a commitment to work at building up human relationships rather than tearing them down. The scar tissue of rejection can be the source of new energy for reconciliation and healing in one's own life and in the lives of others. I have noted again and again that some of the men and women like Tim and Laurie, whom I have met in divorce ministry and who have experienced the most painful rejection, became in time the best healers of others who are rejected.

Resentment

"*I*'m worried, Father, about Sue. She just sits there at our meetings, and mostly doesn't say anything; when she does speak she's really bitter. I get the feeling that she's just smoldering with resentment and anger. What can we do?"

This young man who worried about Sue had analyzed the problem fairly well. I knew Sue and had talked to her several times; she was rusting away with resentment. This can be one of the toughest problems of the divorce recovery process. Sue suffered from her resentment—she seemed paralyzed and unable to move along; she resisted the advice and encouragement of others in the group; she volunteered negative comments whenever she spoke. She seemed listless and lacking in enthusiasm for anything or anyone. Yet she kept coming to meetings—and that was a sign of hope.

Resentment may be less frightening and less visible than the violent outburst of anger, but it is no less destructive. Resentment comes when people like Sue are angry and frustrated with the people and institutions on which they have depended. It can be centered on a former spouse, parents, friends, the Church, or the American way of life; there seems to be no way out and so the resentment simmers. The resentful are usually more unhappy than they realize; they will spend a lot of time pointing out how poor most marriages are today, brood over the stupidity of people where they work, or make caustic comments about people in the Church. Sue seemed unable to do anything to help herself, and seemed caught in a negative trap.

"Why should this have happened to me, Father?" Sue asked me when we sat down to talk. "I was always a good Catholic girl. I didn't sleep around before I was married. When I was a kid, dating more than one guy was considered promiscuity. I always did what you were supposed to do. Why me?" We talked about anger as an expectable part of the grieving process after divorce, and how it is a necessary stage in working through the past. These angry feelings had left her feeling isolated and cut-off. We talked about resentment and how it dwells on injuries endured in the failed marriage, and dwells on every oversight or thoughtless act since. We discussed how resentment was damaging both Sue's thinking processes and her spiritual processes.

"It damages one's whole outlook," I suggested, "by continually focusing on the hurts one has endured, without letting one open oneself to new perspectives and new people." Sue began to see that she had been unwilling to share her own experiences and thus gain from the natural sharing which is part of support group gatherings. "Sharing requires trust and vulnerability, but you, Sue, seem to have been incapable of either recently. You seem to be looking for new material to feed your negative feelings, which puts others on the defensive."

We talked about the damage brought to the spiritual part of one's life by resentment, because spiritual growth most of all requires us to take off our armor and open our hearts to God's healing Spirit. Spiritual growth requires openness to God and others, a willingness to listen, to be affected by what others may suggest, and to begin to adjust destructive behavior. Spiritual growth means that we try to listen to the voice of God speaking to us from within, and through the familiar voices of friends and even strangers.

I was talking on in this way when suddenly Sue broke down

and began to sob uncontrollably. The ache of her tears filled the silence for only a few minutes, but it seemed like an hour.

"It hurts so much, Father," she finally blurted out. "I've *had* to look out for Number One. Nobody else seemed to care. I've been hurt so badly I could scream! You can't believe how much I tried to make that marriage work, and how wronged I felt when he walked out. I just can't get over it. The hurt goes deeper than deep. I've *had* to build this wall around myself, because I'm never going to let myself get hurt like this again. I may not be much, but I'm all I've got."

Sue went on and shared many searing details of her failed marriage. I could see that her self-worth had hit rock bottom, and it became clear that she felt there was no way out. She said she went over the past again and again—reliving old hurts—and at this point she could see no future for herself. She recognized that the only time she felt better was when she voiced her anger and distrust—they were the only feelings she could muster. "My anger, at least, makes me feel alive!"

She went on for well over an hour, and I sat there and listened. I knew there were no brilliant words I could say which could take away all this pain, but I hoped that by listening with love I could help her experience the fact that she was a person of real value. We talked like this for a number of times over the coming weeks, and gradually Sue began to risk with a friend and her support group and share with them more of her story. She was amazed at how well they listened and how much better she felt when she could get things off her chest. The relationships began to deepen, and the resentment, over a period of weeks, slowly began to subside. I experienced with Sue, as never before, how much just being with a person and listening can be healing.

There was no one thing that helped bring Sue around, but many things and many people over many months. Sue began to see that letting go of the anger which causes resentment comes only when one has begun to see a more positive future for oneself. One day Sue said to me: "I was praying yesterday and realized that Thanksgiving was just a week away. I asked myself if I had anything to give thanks for this year, and surprisingly the more I thought about it, the more I began to see that I had much to be grateful for. I was surviving, I had friends, I was beginning to feel closer to God, and even beginning to feel some healthy distance on my marriage."

We talked for a long while about gratitude. I suggested that gratitude can help us untie the knots that have bound us to the past, and can enable us to see new possibilities and new hopes for ourselves. Gratitude means being able to say thanks for my life even though it hasn't turned out the way I planned; thanks for my kids even though they're not superstars and have their own problems too; thanks that I have friends now I never would have met if all this had not happened; thanks that I'm beginning to come through all this older, wiser, better, deeper.

Sue told of a breakthrough moment at a support group meeting the previous night. A young man, a newcomer, was talking about his former wife, and even though he tried to smile the anger was flaming in his eyes. Sue found herself coaxing him to share more of his story, and realized she was listening, quietly, while he built a formidable case against his former wife. All of a sudden it struck her how far she had come. "I used to be in that place," she said to herself. "Thank God I've moved." Yet she felt very close to him, and chatted with him over coffee during the break; she found herself counseling him not to become bitter. "You need your anger now," she stated gently, "but stick around and you'll find in time it will lessen and give way to something better."

Some weeks later I received a letter from Sue, thanking me for "just being there and listening when I was at my worst." She wrote that it wasn't easy yet—she still had her down days—but daily she was taking significant steps to put together a new life. She shared with me some lines from the English playwright George Bernard Shaw which she found herself rereading many times:

> This is the true joy in life, being used for a purpose recognized by yourself as a mighty one; being a force of nature instead of a feverish, selfish little clod of ailments and grievances, complaining that the world will not devote itself to making you happy.
>
> I am of the opinion that my life belongs to the whole community, and, as long as I live, it is my privilege to do for it whatever I can.
>
> I want to be thoroughly used up when I die, for the harder I work, the more I live. I rejoice in life for its own sake. Life is no "brief candle" to me. It is a sort of splendid torch which I have got hold of for the moment, and I want to make it burn as brightly as possible before handing it on to future generations.

Blame

"*I* blame my former husband," Mary said. "He never took the marriage seriously; he was a momma's boy, and had to have everything his own way. I never should have married him. He's with another woman now, and he's acting like a little boy."

"I blame my ex-wife. Frankly, she became 'liberated,' " Tom, Mary's former husband, sighed. "Nothing I did measured up. I was a male-chauvinist bully. I was relieved when she left and said she didn't want to be married anymore."

"I blame the Church," Bill said. "If I hadn't been raised such a sexually mixed-up person with all that guilt and fear, I might have had a chance in my marriage. We just never got it on track, and the bad experiences just piled up to such an extent we couldn't bear each other anymore."

"I blame the war in Vietnam," Sally, Bill's former wife, insisted. "My husband was a great guy when he went off to the war; he returned an emotional mess. His nerves were shot, he couldn't hold a job, he'd fly off into tantrums at the littlest thing. I just couldn't take it anymore, and we separated."

The list goes on. There seems to be an endless collection of persons, places and things that are held to be responsible for divorce, and there's some truth in all of them.

Some people were just not ready for marriage; they were too young, too inexperienced, too immature. In the U.S. couples who marry before they're twenty have a three times greater chance of getting divorced than those who marry after twenty. If there is a pre-marital pregnancy associated with a teenage marriage, the chances are 9 out of 10 that the marriage will end in divorce. The younger people are, the more likely they seem to marry because of some romantic infatuation, and the less likely they are to appreciate the financial, emotional, and interpersonal resources that a lasting marriage requires. The age of entrance into marriage has been going up over the last generation, and families and the Church are doing more and more to discourage early marriage. Who's to blame when a young marriage doesn't work? Certainly the young couple insisted on marrying, but the contemporary passage to adulthood in this society today with maturity coming later, and the lack of resources to assist early marrieds, are factors that have a role too. It's hard to pinpoint the blame.

Some people choose partners almost totally unsuited for lasting marriage. This is another aspect of the romantic illusion, where couples blind themselves to weaknesses in one another, or do not know each other long enough to test compatibility. One researcher friend of mine claims that the best indicator of success in marriage today is a common value system. This means that, despite all the many differences in language, ethnic background and religious upbringing that have shaped the couple, they generally have the same outlook on life and hold the same things important. Testing whether two people have enough common ground on which to build a relationship may demand much longer courtships and a much more honest and probing relationship than was thought necessary in the past. Who's to blame when such a marriage doesn't work and a couple simply gives up after several years, admitting that they can't even agree what day of the week it is? Certainly no one forced them to marry, but the changing social, cultural and religious influences

on marriage were not understood by them, and they had little
help in figuring out what marriage required today. In such cases
it's hard to pinpoint blame.

Some couples discover after some years that they are each
looking for something entirely different from marriage. One expects much more by way of companionship, intimacy, just being
together, while one's spouse is uncomfortable with those things
and prefers the active, busy world of travel and work. There was
a time when we would have assumed that it was the woman who
wanted the first and the man who wanted the second. But that's
not always true anymore. It's not always that these two people
can't stand each other—it's not always the presence of negative
features which drive them apart; it may be more that they're not
on the same wave length; they walk to the beat of a different
drummer; they react to the simplest things very differently.
Some observers say we are suffering from a crisis of rising expectations in marriage; never before have so many people expected so much from their marriages and their marriage
partners—accordingly, never before have so many people been
unhappy. In another age it would have seemed that people with
such complaints were making a mountain out of a molehill.
How, some would ask, can people who have so much going for
them, who are not worried about money and jobs, be so unhappy? Why don't they just shape up and make a go of it?

At some point these dissatisfied couples just seem to wear
out or burn out or decide it's no longer worth the effort. Sometimes another person comes along whom they are attracted to
and find more in common with. We may argue as Christians
that such differences are surmountable and that people can
change and that satisfying marriages can be negotiated, but
those arguments often can't seem to reverse a course of separation which is quietly and inexorably underway. Who's to blame?
The one who walks out may be said to be responsible, but what
about the other who may have been adamant and unyielding and

set the stage? What about the new appetites for personal fulfillment and the new expectations of happiness that are such powerful magnets in today's culture? Aren't they to blame?

Some people give a lot of thought to marriage, get to know the other person fairly well, are old enough and financially secure, and seem to be ready for marriage according to any barometer. But then they marry and find that their spouse has serious emotional problems which were never evident during the courtship. It may well be that the tensions and pressures of marriage accentuated behaviors which were fairly dormant prior to marriage. A wife turns out to be depressed most of the time, and possibly even chemically dependent. She seemed sexually responsive before marriage, but now she has lost all interest in sexual relations. Or the husband took a drink or two with the boys before marriage, but now his drinking is hurting him on the job, and there are indications that he may be alcoholic. He seemed easy to get along with before marriage, but now he is touchy about his authority and insists on getting his way; he has even become physically threatening when confronted with ordinary demands. Many individuals seem to go psychologically downhill after marriage; they simply do not seem to develop the interpersonal emotional resources that marriage requires. Others go along pretty well for a time, but some dramatic stress— loss of a child, loss of a job, physical sickness—seems to change them, and they become like unknown persons. We live in an emotionally demanding society in which many stressful factors beyond the control of marriage partners seem to wound their fragile relationship and pull them apart. Professional psychological evaluation may suggest that one partner could never be married to anyone without undergoing some significant personal change. Who's to blame?

When one examines the stories of failed marriages, there is always a lot of blame to go around. Often immediately after a difficult separation it seems so clear that the other person is to blame. Blaming may be an inevitable response to pain, and a kind of knee-jerk response to marital failure, but in the long run it is always the enemy of genuine recovery. (Not that a clear assessment of what went wrong in the relationship and the role of each in the failure of the marriage is not an important learning experience in time; self-knowledge may be an important ingredient in personal growth.) Blaming which lets oneself completely off the hook and lays the burden of fault and guilt completely on the other person is not personally beneficial. The other person may well have been responsible for the immediate cause of separation—walking out for another person, domestic violence, neglect, refusal to seek help. Yet there are always important areas in every failed marriage which suggest personal self-exploration and growth: Why did I marry a person like this? How did I deal with the stress in the marriage? What does this failed marriage tell me about myself and my own need for personal growth?

Just as it isn't profitable to blame the other person, so it isn't profitable to blame oneself either. Some people falsely let the other off the hook completely and punish themselves with fault and guilt. All marriages involve two people, and it is the unique interaction of these two particular people with their own personal characteristics which make the relationship untenable. Genuine personal growth after divorce involves a realistic assessment of what went wrong in the marriage; one needs to understand what this sad experience tells me about myself—what my needs are now as a human person, and what this self-knowledge tells me about my future.

Mary was fortunate to attend a Beginning Experience weekend. She told me later that the process of the weekend brought her for the first time to a concrete realization of what she had contributed to the failure of her marriage. "It was hard to accept," she said, "but I recognized that I had an illusion of what a husband should be—very much a carbon copy of my own father whom I adored—and Tom could never measure up. He had his own problems, but maybe if we both had been more open and accepting, we could have dealt more realistically with each other. Even if we could not have worked things out, at least we could have parted more honestly and without so much bitterness."

Bill went on the same weekend, and said he mightily resisted those sessions which confronted his steel-plated self-justification. "They're not going to get me to blame myself," he resolved early on. But gradually after many hours of conversation he found himself melting. "I began to see that I had my career, my life-style, my way a wife should be, my kind of marriage, and on and on. I never moved from 'I' to 'we'; I never opened myself to the possibility that we could build something new and different together. I was just too caught up in myself to face the personal sacrifice and change that a relationship requires. I can see now I was kind of dumb."

Whatever may be the complex reasons a marriage fails, blame with all that it implies about psychological punishment or scapegoating is always enormously counterproductive. In true recovery, blame must give way to mutual understanding, mutual responsibility, self-knowledge and personal growth.

Depression

It hits like the storm in an Arizona sky,
    it comes and goes almost in the blink of an eye.
What are these feelings that keep coming and going
    like the tides in the sea:
What on earth is happening to me?

Can it be I'm not coping as well as I thought?
    I keep working, and going to school
    to try to fill my head with sensible tools.
But in the middle of this my brains and emotions
    come to a screeching halt.
They start churning and twisting beyond my control,
    then the next thing I know I'm lost again
    in some large empty hole.

I see where my work is affected by all this,
    yet when I try to straighten it out,
I only seem to cause a bigger mess.
When will it end, all these storms and high tides?
    When can I say the forecast
    is bright and sunny skies?
I know the answer is soon in coming,
    but it's the between now and then
    that isn't worth living.

Oh, but to be a caterpillar and roll up in a cocoon,
    or a big grizzly bear and hibernate for the winter.
These things may be wished for,
    but are never to come about,
So in the end we must face whatever life dishes out.

This poem was shared by a young woman with a group of us at a retreat last year. The writer is 25 and twice divorced; she has been struggling with depression since her most recent divorce a year before.

Depression is a familiar companion of those who experience marriage breakdown. Feeling low, unable to get up in the morning, unable to perform ordinary household chores—this is depression. A pervasive and almost free-floating anger is part of depression—anger at self, anger at a former spouse, anger at parents, anger at children, anger at friends, anger at God, on and on. For some the anger after divorce becomes an engine which drives them to put together a new life situation for themselves, get in better physical shape, go back to school, make new friends, take a more challenging job. But for many the anger is turned in on themselves. What's wrong with me that I ever married this person? How could I have been so stupid? Why didn't I listen to what others said? What's ever going to become of me? I know I'll never feel better. Why has everyone turned against me? I know I'm just going to drag through life. Why are people laughing at me? I know I'll never experience love again.

Such anger turned on oneself can be like a corrosive acid eating away at the potential of recovery, blinding one to one's own gifts, immobilizing one's energies and gifts.

Several years ago I received this letter:

Last night I couldn't sleep again, and lay there feeling my nerves on edge and that familiar, groaning inner voice telling me: You're no good. I've been battling

> those feelings day and night, and I don't seem to be
> winning. Yet I know I can't give up. I try to meditate
> on the Scripture: "He has carved us in the palm of his
> hand and knows us by name." I try to tell myself that
> I'm a good person, that having failed at marriage is not
> the end of the world or the end of life for me. I'm be-
> ginning to realize that I always had to be perfect, and
> couldn't stand the thought of coming in second. Isn't
> the best I'm able to do enough? Yet the pain and the
> fear in the pit of my stomach comes back and I lie there
> unable to sleep.

These painful sentences capture so precisely the agony of
the depressed divorcing person—a struggle to fight self-destructive impulses and construct a new vision which allows one to be
imperfect, flawed, human.

Some depression is part of the divorce transition for everyone; when the depression lingers for months on end, I always
suggest that the person seek medical attention. Severe depression can be terribly self-destructive, and its worst effects can be
softened and even reversed by good medical care. A solid Christian response to such a debilitating, emotional illness is to seek
appropriate care. God certainly wants us to help ourselves this
way.

Depression and anger are a normal part of the grieving
process. They won't go away with one conversation or one pill,
nor should they. For the divorcing need time to mourn their
losses, time to let go, time to sort out their pain. That time is a
mixed and confused time, a forward and backward time, an up
and down time. Anger and depression are always part of it. I've
known people who tried to hurry themselves out of depression,
not realizing that the breakdown of a marriage is a devastating
loss. They had to learn to be patient with our normal, slow capacity to heal. Someone once said that losing a spouse by death

or divorce is like losing a leg—it takes a long time to learn to walk again with one leg.

For those whose depression is mild and tied to the stress of the early weeks and months after separation, a prayerful, Christian reflection on failure can be most helpful. Fr. Jack Finnegan likes to insist that we Christians have a great theology of failure but never use it. Wasn't Jesus himself a failure? On that first Good Friday as he hung there on that cross, he did not look like a great success. His disciples must have felt that he had failed and that all their dreams about a new Israel had been reduced to ashes. His ministry had been so brief. He had barely begun to teach, make an impact, change the hearts and minds of the people. Sure he attracted great crowds, but as the week of his death showed, the crowds could be fickle, saluting him with a parade on Sunday and then screaming for his execution on Friday. He had healed the blind and the lame and the deaf and the crippled, yet he had barely touched the unfortunate and suffering of his homeland. His journeys had covered only the very limited terrain of this postage-stamp country. There was so much more to do! A sense of promise nipped in the bud seems to pour out of his lament on the night before he died, "Father, if it be your will, let this chalice pass away." He didn't want to die; he wanted to go on serving. It seemed such a waste. "Not my will, but yours be done."

His Father snatched victory from the jaws of defeat. He saw Jesus' love, his fidelity, his perseverance, his obedience, and raised him to new life. "Therefore God has highly exalted him and bestowed on him the name which is above every name, so that at the name of Jesus every knee should bow, in heaven and on earth and under the earth, and every tongue confess that Jesus Christ is Lord, to the glory of God the Father" (Phil 2:9–11).

His failure, his death, his shame changed all human history. St. Paul learned the lesson of his defeat so well; again and again he boasts of his infirmities. "When I am weak, then I am strong!" Great saints over the centuries learned that same lesson—out of a dark night of the soul much like contemporary depression often came new life in Christ.

How to harness the anger that is defeating one and turn it into energy for growth and new life is the secret to overcoming depression. Ron told me that he would stand each morning, look at himself in the mirror, and repeat ten times, "God loves you. God doesn't make junk!" The core of the ministry of Jesus was announcing to those who had been beaten down and nearly destroyed that they were loved by his Father. In fact, he insisted that those who suffered the most were closest to his Father. "The Lord hears the cry of the poor," the prophets of the Old Testament cried again and again. Jesus began his ministry by reading from the prophet Isaiah in the synagogue at Nazareth: "The Spirit of the Lord is upon me, because he has anointed me to preach good news to the poor. He has sent me to proclaim release to the captives and recovering of sight to the blind, to set at liberty those who are oppressed" (Luke 4:18–20).

The poor he speaks of are not just the materially poor, the blind are not just the physically blind, and the captives are not just those in prison. He comes to set free those who suffer emotionally, are blinded by life's tragedies and cannot discern their own worth, are captives of powerful feelings which tell them that life is not worth living. He comes to turn that anger which cripples and destroys into a force for personal growth and development, to transform those emotions which bind into forces for friendship and service of others, to untie the knots of self-destructive pain which imprison.

Dr. Karl Menninger likes to give this advice to the discouraged:

People are unreasonable, illogical, self-centered.
　　Love them anyway.

If you do good, people will accuse you of selfish, ulterior
motives.
Do good anyway.
If you are successful, you will win false friends and true
enemies.
Try to be successful anyway.
The good you do today will be forgotten tomorrow.
Do it anyway.
Honesty and frankness make you vulnerable.
Be honest and frank anyway.
People favor underdogs, but they follow the top dogs.
Fight for some underdogs anyway.
What you spend years building may be destroyed overnight.
Build anyway.
Give the world the best you have, and you'll get kicked in
the teeth.
Give the world the best you have, anyway.

Most of all in fighting depression we need other people.
Depression tempts us to withdraw, isolate ourselves, languish.
It tells us that no one could care, no one could make a difference. I've seen people drag themselves into divorced Catholics
group meetings, and I've seen them visibly pick up amid the give
and take of the group. I've seen sensitive, alert group members
nudge and poke those who are down, and with gentle concern
and a little well-laced humor bring a grudging smile to their
faces. I've seen group members follow up on depressed people
with phone calls and invitations to movies and picnics in the
park. I've seen friends get together and straighten up apart-
ments, fill out income tax forms, and pay bills for hurting
friends. "The whole idea of compassion," the monk Thomas
Merton writes, "is based on a keen awareness of the inter-
dependence of all living beings; we are all part of one another,
and all involved in one another."

When one of us hurts, we all hurt. When one of us is depressed, we are all depressed. It's that kind of solidarity that has made support groups so successful in lifting out of depression many recently separated persons. Millie, a psychiatric nurse, says, "You can't rely on psychiatry alone, nor can you rely on prayer and friends alone. But all together, they can help you open yourself to God, and can help the healing begin."

Many times people ask me if I get depressed working so much with depressed people. I always tell them that the opposite is the case. Maybe it's a matter of the glass half-empty or the glass half-full—a matter of how you look at things. But when I see someone depressed during the divorce transition I prefer to see the loving, whole person struggling to come out. It's like the story of the little boy who saw a large block of marble in the sculptor's studio one day; returning weeks later he saw a great lion sitting on the pedestal where the block of marble had been. "How did you find that lion in the marble?" the boy asked the sculptor. How do new people come out of depressed people? The loving touch of the divine sculptor assisted by the loving touch of many earthly sculptors helps depressed persons to find new life in themselves. That's what my experience has been—seeing so often the revitalized people who have begun to live after divorce reaching out to the newly hurting. That's not depressing. It's exhilarating!

Loneliness

*L*inda put it so succinctly: "I felt as though some-one had outlined me with a black grease pencil. I was aware of every inch of my body, every thought racing in my head. While I was listening to my breathing, I felt so out of touch with oth-ers, so isolated, so alone. I wanted someone to talk to, to pour it all out to, but I knew no one would care to listen. I felt as though I was on a desert island, and there was no Robinson Crusoe in sight."

Loneliness is an inevitable part of the divorce transition. Bob Weiss, author of the book *Loneliness*, says that the loneli-ness of the divorced is uniquely painful. If someone is married and a spouse goes away on a business trip, the two miss each other; yet they can connect on the phone, and the loneliness is relieved. They can count the days until he or she returns, and the expectancy lessens the loneliness. But the divorced don't know anyone who can overcome their aloneness. The pain is heightened by the existence of that someone, a former spouse, who once provided personal security and companionship, but that person is gone now, and would be the last person on earth one would think of contacting.

Some people report missing their former spouse, and won-der what's wrong with them that they are thinking so much about someone they can't bear to be with. This happens often to the recently separated. We know that all marriages, even ones that aren't successful, generate attachment between husband

and wife. Years of living together, sharing many of the practical aspects of marriage, raising kids together, sleeping together—all these experiences develop attachment bonds. When two people part, almost inevitably they miss one another, even though they know down deep that getting together again will not help. Sometimes couples mistake this lingering attachment for revived affection and attempt a reconciliation, only to discover fairly quickly that it is a mistake.

Separation for both men and women confronts them with a totally new life situation—living as an unmarried person. Many men and women had little independent life experience before marrying, or if they did, it was so long ago that they now find themselves totally unprepared for the many practical challenges of shaping a new living situation. Raising children as a single parent or relating to them as an absent parent, stretching income to cover two residences, relating to family and friends as a separated person, coping with difficult feelings of failure and fear about the future—all these powerful, nagging feelings can contribute to loneliness. "There doesn't seem to be anyone else who understands kids, or has ever been divorced in this town, or could possibly know how to fix these storm windows."

Linda put it this way: "There's an inevitable desire to find someone else to fill the void, someone who could make me feel better, make me feel loved, someone to just be there—to share a cup of coffee with, listen to one's daily misadventures. But where do you meet such a person? Wouldn't most people be bored by my petty struggles? I'm not even sure how men and women who aren't married relate to each other anymore."

Bob Weiss says there are two aspects to the loneliness of the separated and divorced. First there is emotional loneliness which is brought about by the absence of the intimate attachment of marriage, and, second, there is social loneliness, which is brought about by the collapse of the network of friends and associates who were part of the fabric of one's married life. He insists that people need both emotional and social attachments to prevent loneliness; one cannot compensate for the other. The emotional loneliness of the recently separated and divorcing is heightened by the inevitable fact that they are self-focused and self-conscious and have no intimate partner. Yet human well-being also necessitates being involved successfully with many other people. The separated search desperately for relationships to ease their loneliness, but they work against themselves by often being overly sensitive to any sign of rejection. They often back out of relationships because a new friend turns out to be less than ideally accepting or ideally happy. They're insecure about breaking new ground in relationships.

Some recently separated people find that they're just not very good at starting and maintaining friendships: how to introduce yourself, how to listen, how to start a conversation, how and when to disclose things about oneself, how to be appropriately assertive. Developing realistic expectations about friendships seems to take time.

Most of us are raised to relate to people of the opposite sex as part of the mating/dating game. Someone is only worth spending time with if there's some prospect of marriage coming out of the relationship. This means that we usually don't relate seriously to people who are much older, or much younger, or of very different backgrounds and interests, or people of different cultures or religions. A special opportunity after marital separation is the possibility of relating to a wider variety of people, and even coming close to some, whom one would never think of marrying. The close relationships one needs will more likely come if one is relating widely and not expecting one or two new relationships to make all the difference.

Divorce support groups can be a very important way of coping with the inevitable loneliness after separation, because they can provide a new network of friends, a varied collection of people, wider than the more limited social circle that was part of married life. Managing loneliness will come by persisting at meetings, taking interest in others, following up on good encounters that have occurred. Taking advantage of the social opportunities that a group sponsors may also be an important way of lifting one's spirits and introducing some playfulness back into one's life. We Americans are busy, hard-working, ambitious people who by and large are not good at giving ourselves the relaxed time and space necessary to get to know other people and build friendships. The time after separation and divorce can be a special time for reshaping the interpersonal patterns of one's previous life.

The Church has always proposed that the separated and divorced should immediately embrace a single life. My experience suggests that there's great wisdom in that. To think that there is some magic someone out there who's going to be my closest friend or marry me again soon may be a destructive illusion. Committing oneself to developing the personal resources to be "alone yet all together" is one of the great challenges facing the separated and divorced. It's often said that being alone is not the same as being lonely. Learning to be alone with oneself and to enjoy one's company is important for all people, but it is a key to personal development after divorce. It doesn't come easily—it takes great time, patience and effort, but the rewards can be enormous.

We read in the Scriptures that Jesus was often alone. Again and again in the Gospels we find him stealing time alone to pray. We see in his life that solitude is not an escape from relationships, but rather the peaceful place where true intimacy with God and others and especially oneself can begin to develop. Being able to be alone really teaches us how to be with others. If we are restless, frazzled, full of nervous chatter, people will soon avoid our company, or at best tolerate it. Think of people whose company you enjoy—I'm sure they're easy-going, in touch with themselves, interested in others. It's obvious as you get to know them that they have a center, a place where they meet themselves, a place where they meet God. For when we work at being alone, we can't help but begin to meet ourselves, and in meeting ourselves, we can't help but meet the God who made us. God is certainly out there in the farthest reaches of the galaxies, and the splendor of his creation can wrap us in awe. Yet when we go deep into ourselves, down to the very edges of our being, we find him there. "In him we live and move and have our being." The God we meet in the depths is the God of peace and quiet and stillness. As the psalmist says, "Be still and know that I am God."

Learning to be alone, to embrace solitude, takes some practice. We need to turn off the car radio, turn off the TV, take off into the woods alone, or drop into a quiet chapel. Sometimes we need to sit on our hands and give ourselves two minutes more when we feel the urge to stop wasting time and do something more productive.

In solitude we learn that we are not alone. We begin to sense the bonds that tie us to one another and to God, to see that being with others in loving, supportive community is a gift from God. Solitude is time apart which makes time together more meaningful. It helps us see that the deep human ties of brotherhood and sisterhood preceded all separation and alienation. It is the source of gentleness, tenderness, peacefulness, healing.

Solitude is the place where God reveals himself to us as God-within-us, as the God who is the source, center, and purpose of our existence, as the God who gives himself to us with unlimited love, and the God who wants to be loved by us in return with all our hearts. The prophet Elijah, when he searched for God's presence, did not find him in the mighty wind, the earthquake, or the raging fire, but rather in the gentle breeze and the still small voice within. In meeting God there at the depths, we know that we are loved, that we are valuable, that we are precious, that we are not alone.

Linda summed it up: "It took me some time before I realized how lonely I was when I was married. Now that I've moved out of that marriage, through much blood, sweat and tears, I've learned to deal with loneliness. I learned that there wasn't something wrong with me, but rather that I was being called to a deeper experience of God and of myself."

Endings

Remember when we were kids and we never wanted summer to end; we never wanted the Christmas tree to come down; we never wanted an ice cream cone to be licked away; we never wanted bedtime to come. Our parents always tried to assure us that there would be another summer, another Christmas, another ice cream cone, another tomorrow. We took their word for it—we had to, but oh how we wanted to hold onto that moment. Who knew what the future would bring?

Few of us are very good at endings—saying farewell to friends, leaving a first job, moving out of the house we grew up in, finding something to say when a loved one dies, or admitting that a marriage is over. We naturally like to hold onto persons and things who have meant something to us, even if they've slipped away. We pore over old photo albums and souvenirs from trips which bring back happier times. Sometimes we get dreamily stuck back there, and have a hard time coming back to reality.

I think we could all learn something about endings from the Church. The Church deals with endings by talking always about beginnings. For example, on that day when we have died and our loved ones carry our mortal remains into the house of God, the priest will sprinkle with water the coffin wrapped in the white cloth and remind us of our beginning at baptism:

All of us who were baptized into Christ Jesus were baptized into his death. By baptism into his death we

41

were buried together with him, so that just as Christ
was raised from the dead by the glory of the Father, we
too might live a new life. For if we have been united
with him by likeness to his death, so shall we be united
with him by likeness to his resurrection (Rom 6:3–8).

The basic message of the Christian funeral rite, which is a
basic message for all Christian living, is captured succinctly in
the Preface of the Eucharistic Prayer: "For the Christian life is
not ended, merely changed." For the believer then there are no
real endings, just changes. Each beginning leads to an ending
which is really the prelude to another beginning. Being able to
change means that one has grasped this basic truth, is able to see
new beginnings in endings. Cardinal Newman, the great nineteenth century English convert, said: "To be a Christian is to
change, and to be holy is to have changed often."

Being able to change means being able to let go of the past
and embrace a largely unknown future. It is an act of hope, of
courage, of risk. Being able to change doesn't mean that we blot
out the past, but rather that we ease out of the past, free ourselves from its grip, and let it become a freeing memory. We
need memory to enrich and enliven our present situation, re-
minding us of friends and strengths and little accomplishments.
But memory is only a friend when it nudges us into the future.
Some hold onto the past as a way of beating themselves down,
tormenting themselves with past defeats. Being able to change
means we've begun to put those demons of the past to rest, begun to forgive ourselves, and begun to bring forward those
proven resources which can help us move on.

Christian growth for the divorced is tied to the ability to
embrace change and move through difficult endings to new beginnings. Just as the funeral rite reminds us that because of baptism the ending of our earthly life is but the prelude to entering
eternal life, the divorced must be reminded that the end of a

marriage can be the prelude to a new human existence and a new Christian identity.

We know that not everyone grows and becomes a more together person after divorce. There's something of the kid in all of us that resists endings and change. As we get older, we often seem to get better at blocking and standing still and resisting the future. We learn not to finish sentences, to live with our energy tied up in old battles, and to hold onto failed relationships. We just can't terminate, let go, face endings, embrace change, believe in tomorrow.

For those who feel stuck in this process of changing and moving on, I suggest a meditation on change in the life of Jesus, a man who dealt with endings well, who changed often. Jesus left father and mother, in answer to his Father's call, and went about announcing the coming of the Kingdom of God. Nothing seems to have ever made up for the loss of his childhood home, for in his ministry he became truly homeless. "The birds have their nests, the foxes their dens, yet the Son of Man has nowhere to lay his head." Yet he seems to have moved through that loss and found himself at home with the most unlikely companions, welcomed joyfully into the residences of outcasts and sinners.

This is not to suggest that endings were easy for him. When he learned that his dear friend Lazarus had died, he sobbed uncontrollably. Life without Lazarus must have seemed almost unbearable. Yet he accepted the death and went to the tomb to pray for him. Almost overcome with grief, he shouts out the name of Lazarus, and to the astonishment of all with him, Lazarus comes forth, prefiguring the passage from death to life again which lay ahead of Jesus.

Each day Jesus placed himself in his Father's hands, and each day brought new separations, new uncertainties, new struggles. Yet each day he grew and changed and each day the Father opened his eyes to an ever-expanding vision of his mission. Resting faithfully in his Father's embrace, he was able to empty himself and live freely until the day he faced the final change, the ending on the cross. This ending became, in his Father's love, the beginning of new life in the resurrection. Because he had embraced change all through his life—resting securely in the abiding memory of his Father's love and trusting in his kingdom to come—he was able to face the greatest change, the greatest ending of all.

I've talked to many divorced people who thought that their lives were over when their marriages came to an end; they were tormented by memories from the past and were paralyzed about facing an uncertain future. The trauma of broken marriage brings such paralysis for a time to all who face its fears and terrors. It takes time to sort out the past, recover enduring strengths and let go of failed dreams. It takes time to take hold of the present and begin to marshal resources for making it on a day-to-day basis. The future at first seems bleak and threatening; it seems beyond human possibility to begin to sort out the dimensions of a new life. Change is so hard to embrace.

One needs many allies at this difficult time, especially loved ones and good friends who can support one through this demanding process of sifting and rebuilding. A Christian perspective on it all, one like that I've just tried to outline, can be an important resource at this time. Our faith tells us that life has not ended but merely changed. Our faith tells us that the loving resources of a God who has been with us from the beginning will be with us through this terrifying transition. Our faith helps us disenthrall ourselves from the past and begin to see the light of dawn. Our faith tells us that with God's help and our own grit and tenacity we can become new persons—not one who has erased the past, but one who sees it now with deromanticized clarity and honest self-assessment. Our faith helps us reach out to the new companions for rebuilding our lives which the Spirit sends our way. Our faith enables us to believe that we can become an older, wiser, more loving, better person than we ever were before.

I've met many people who look back years later and see how confining and suffocating their marriage relationship was, and how they have since shaped a more independent and more satisfying life for themselves. They look back now on the tidy Catholicism of their childhood with all its ready answers which has crumbled away, yet find themselves now living a far more adult Christian life. They were terrified in moving away from the security of a marriage which, even though it was lifeless, promised certain protections and status; they now find themselves happier as a single person or married again than they ever dreamed possible.

Our lives may not have the happy endings that storybooks like to chart; in fact, our lives may have many endings, not all of them happy. Change often seems to be our constant companion, leaving us often breathless and weary. Our faith tells us that if we see the hope of beginning again in each ending then we will have grasped at its deepest what it is to be a Christian, a follower of him who changed often, and in so doing showed us what it is to be holy.

Recovery

"*H*ow long does it take to recover from a divorce?"
I've posed that question to hundreds of groups of divorced Catholics. The answers are always varied. Some say a year, some say
a lifetime, some say never, some say three years, some say more
than four, some say it depends. It depends on the length of the
marriage, they say, or on what the marriage was like, or on how
many problems followed the divorce, or on the kind of help available. There is some truth in all these things. There is a way in
which people always carry the pain of divorce with them in some
respect the rest of their lives; how could one just erase the most
significant life decision ever made, and the most painful life experience one ever endured? Some people do have much more to
contend with than others after separation—more kids, more
physical and emotional problems, less money, fewer emotional
supports. Some divorced couples relate fairly well to each other
and cooperate realistically and maturely in raising their children. Others cannot tolerate each other's presence even after
many years.

The key word in my question is "recover." I always propose
that you have to define the word before you can suggest how long
recovery takes. Many psychologists say that a person is recovered
when he or she has moved from the emotional depths of the moment when the decision to divorce is made (or when one is informed about a spouse's decision to divorce) to a point where
they have distanced themselves from the failed marriage and

have established a viable, independent life for themselves. Recovery doesn't mean that there aren't any lingering stresses and wearying complications that come with the fact of being divorced; it means rather that one gets up in the morning and feels confident that one will be able to handle fairly well whatever may come one's way that day. No bets are made about tomorrow! To be recovered means that one has moved beyond the rollercoaster mood swings, the free-floating, uninvited anxiety, the terror about the future, and the bottomless loneliness, and arrived at a new plateau on which one has acquired some confidence in one's own resources. One now takes pride in holding life and limb together for oneself and possibly one's children, where one knows that he or she could never go back to the marriage—one has grown too much, changed too much. Establishing such an autonomous life is considered by many the meaning of recovery after divorce.

Even though autonomy may look very different for different people and some of its triumphs look fairly modest to an outsider, even though different people deal with different issues at different levels of intensity all through the process, we seem to observe that no matter how many variables there are, it takes the average person some three to five years to move to single autonomy after separation.

"Three years ago I came to this retreat and felt that he was full of crap when he gave this stuff about three to five years," Barbara volunteered at a retreat I gave in Phoenix. "But I had only been separated three months then, and wanted an instant cure; I couldn't listen to this three to five year business. That was three years ago, and I'm back for another weekend, because I've since learned that much of what he said was right on target."

To say that recovery takes three to five years is certainly somewhat arbitrary. Some people do very well after a couple of years, and some never seem to recover adequately—they are as wrapped in pain ten years later as they were on the day they divorced. Some psychologists say that it's better to talk about predictable stages that everyone goes through, and that the duration of the stages varies with different people. I prefer to talk in terms of years, just because it sounds so long; we're such a "quick fix," "instant cure" society that we get very impatient with ourselves when we don't get over things the day we want to get over them. Divorcing people often don't appreciate the depth of the trauma and the extent of the emotional damage they've endured. They often don't recognize how complex the tasks of shaping a new identity and a new life situation are. They often don't see at first the meaning of the social collapse that follows divorce and how hard it is to establish a new network of friends and restructure relationships with family and relatives. They often underestimate the depth of the spiritual crisis which follows marital breakup—What does this all mean? What's going to become of me? Will I ever be happy again? How do I relate to God now? Many aspects of ordinary living which were predictable and comforting when married, like work and Church and raising kids and having some fun, have all now grown complicated and puzzling.

Standing on one's own two feet, building confidence in one's personal and spiritual resources, acquiring comfort with the person one is becoming—all this takes a lot of tenacity and perseverance. No one ever grows in an ever-forward, ever-positive, ever-upward direction; all human growth comes in fits and starts, lurching forward and backward, with setbacks as full of learning as new discoveries. Getting discouraged and fantasizing about running off to Morocco comes with the real estate of divorce. Florence told me that her six kids would some days get to her so badly that she would go down in the basement and pound her son's punching bag. Ted took up jogging and admitted he became quite a fanatic about it because it helped him work off tension and sleep better at night. And Barbara said hello to yellow wax build up and peanut butter sandwich dinners and unmade beds for weeks on end, because survival just became more important than being Homemaker of the Year.

We know now that people who become part of support groups do better in the adjustment period after separation; new friends tend to prod one emotionally, and can provide good, practical advice so that one doesn't have to reinvent the divorce wheel; and they can also give some confidence that one's problems are quite normal, and that one's really not losing one's grip. People come and go in divorce groups, because they have good stretches and bad stretches. That's why it's important for groups to meet regularly all year long at the same place and time, so that those who need support at a particular moment can fall back on the group. Groups need to meet at least twice a month, and weekly if possible, so that the help is available when needed.

There are many helpful books that provide many insightful descriptions of the divorce transition. Some use the grief stages of Dr. Elisabeth Kübler-Ross; others adapt the twelve steps of Alcoholics Anonymous; still others use techniques and interpretations drawn from psychological therapies and religious practices. I feel that whatever approach appeals to a person and seems to work for him should be embraced. No two people go through this arduous time in the same way and at the same speed, and no one approach appeals to everyone.

Spiritual recovery is linked to the same process of recovery, yet its issues can be quite different. The spiritual crisis of the divorcing Catholic focuses around these questions: What happened to the grace of the sacrament? Didn't we receive God's grace to have a lasting marriage on our wedding day? Does this divorce mean that I've offended God and will be punished by him? Didn't God mean us to marry each other from all eternity in his divine plan, and doesn't this divorce mean that we've messed up his plan, and things will never work out right for us again? Is it a sin to ever hope to marry again and find the happiness I dreamed of but never found in this failed marriage? These questions can cause enormous anxiety among divorcing Catholics.

First of all, marriages are not made in heaven, but are made on earth by two human beings. God doesn't choose our marriage partners for us. If he did we would be no more than puppets on a string. The God of Christians is a God who makes us most like himself in giving us freedom to make significant decisions about our lives. We choose our husbands and wives by our very own decision-making. The grace of the sacrament means that God offers us his love and help in developing that life together which will lead husband and wife together to his Kingdom. Many people make bad choices in marrying; others may have made promising enough choices at the beginning, but their marriages turn out to be disasters because of sickness or problems beyond the control of the couple. God's grace never fails us, but he doesn't turn around our faulty decisions; rather, he helps us learn from our mistakes and grow through them. When tragedy strikes, his loving presence is with us to help us salvage our lives and start anew. God does not abandon us because a marriage fails. Even if we are responsible for the breakup of a marriage, even if our own neglect or drunkenness or stupidity fatally destroys a marriage relationship, God does not abandon us, but offers us the help we need to work through the past and build a new life.

I was on a television show where the interviewer said to me, "Let's face it, Father. Aren't you just trying in your work to take off people's backs all the guilt the Church laid on them over the years?" I answered, "I am trying to remove guilt which is false and inappropriate. I've met lots of people who are mired in guilt about things over which they had no power or responsibility. But there are other persons I've met who should feel guilty that their marriage has ended in divorce. They contributed to the breakdown by their own actions. The Church doesn't hit them over the head, but says: Acknowledge your faults, seek forgiveness, and receive the healing love of the Lord. The Church in the sacrament of reconciliation brings freedom from debilitating guilt for those who call on the Lord for help."

God does not punish the divorced; rather, Scripture says that he seeks out the brokenhearted and offers them healing. The Church does not teach that divorce is a sin, even though some may have sinned against God, their spouse or their families at the time of divorce. The Gospel calls those who may have sinned at this time to repentance and pardon and peace from the Lord. When the Lord forgives he wipes away our offenses and holds them against us no longer. The worst punishment I've ever seen divorced people receive is from themselves. The Lord invites us to accept his forgiveness and love and to stop punishing ourselves and begin to love ourselves again.

God's plan is that all of us should be saved and enjoy everlasting peace in his Kingdom. The details of his plan are still being worked out and are beyond our knowing at the present; we do know that when we experience failure or sin in our lives, he invites us to reconciliation and a new start. Again and again he offers us the chance to start anew. His plan shifts and accommodates our weakness and our mess-ups.

Barbara is now five years beyond her divorce and says she is beginning to understand now what recovery has meant for her. She never would have dreamed five years ago how far she would move in the time ahead; she never would have dreamed then that she could work through all the pain and achieve such personal contentment. I swore to the group in Phoenix that I did not plant her at the retreat; if I had known all that had happened to her, I surely would have asked her to come.

Women

"*F*ather, when I was growing up I was somebody's daughter," Julie told me, "then I became somebody's girlfriend, then somebody's fiancée, then somebody's wife. You know what? Now that I've gotten divorced, I think I've finally become somebody!"

Many Catholic women are achieving significant personal autonomy after divorce for the first time in their lives. Like most other American women, Catholic women are admitting that they grew up dreaming about marriage, worried at twenty whether they would become an old maid, and never entertained any other personal life goals than becoming a wife and a mother. Most of their thinking was done for them for most of their lives by others—first their parents, later their husbands. The whole life pattern was reinforced all along by the Church. As Julie put it, "I was a good Catholic girl; I never thought my marriage wouldn't work. Hadn't this all been pre-ordained from eternity? Weren't we supposed to live happily ever after if we each did our part? The problem is, I did my part, and he did his part too—but it didn't work out."

I've sat with many divorced Catholic women like Julie who talked at length about their naiveté before and during their marriages. "When we first started fighting and the freeze set in and we didn't talk for months, I pretended it wasn't happening, because I assumed our marriage would work. I really knew nothing about sex when we got married, and I don't think my husband

52

knew much more. We never seemed to be able to get it together and enjoy it. Babies only seemed to make it more of a problem."

Julie then told me about the annulment of her marriage: "When I was interviewed by a priest at the tribunal about my possible annulment, he asked me why I had ever had four babies in four years when my husband was a compulsive gambler and an alcoholic. I almost hit him. I screamed at him, 'You're the ones who told me I had to have babies. I didn't want the babies all at once, but I was always taught Catholics didn't practice birth control.'

"A number of people tried to talk us out of getting married, but I was just plain thick. It was obvious to everyone else that we didn't have anything in common, and that he was really a boy. I don't know how it lasted six years. It only lasted that long because I was a Catholic and Catholics didn't get divorced.

"I had always been Daddy's little girl, and then I became my husband's little girl. But when I began finally to grow up, to think for myself, and to look for something more from life, it was obvious that my husband couldn't handle it."

Some observers feel that even though divorcing women like Julie may have more than men to overcome after a divorce, in many ways they seem to be doing better in American society today than divorcing men. Women may have a lot of catching up to do in gaining personal independence, but they also have assistance from the women's movement and an array of new educational programs designed for single mothers and working women. I've sensed pride in divorced women when they talk about their struggles and how far they've come.

At many support group meetings and conferences, people wonder why there are so many women present and so few men. First of all, the population of divorced people in the U.S. who have not remarried is not 50–50. Men remarry more quickly, and older divorced men do not live as long as their wives. The U.S. Census Bureau says that over 60% of divorced persons who have not remarried are women. Yet there are still not as many men present as there could be. Men seem to have a harder time coming out publicly and looking for help; women are much more likely to cry on a friend's shoulder, or join a support group, or go to a Church meeting for the divorced. Sometimes women find Church-sponsored events much easier to attend, since they seem safe and the women have fewer social outlets.

I also wonder if men are more fearful of being made to feel guilty by the Church. Men seem afraid that the Church like most people will blame them for a marriage which didn't work; after all men are expected to be more responsible. Many men seem temperamentally less flexible than women and more morally rigid. "Father, I just didn't feel I could live up to the whole package anymore," one man told me, "so I just checked out of the Church." Women seem more able to stay in the Church even while having trouble with parts of it, and they seem more motivated to try to change it.

Men will come to support group meetings if they find that it's not a "women's group" and that men are not always blamed for everything wrong in marriage today. "I never heard of the word 'patriarchy' until a woman dumped it on my head at a meeting and said that all of us controlling, dominating men were impossible to live with." The feminist movement has offered women some powerful analysis of their confused personal and social situation. I like to tell women that I consider myself a feminist; I support everything in the movement which helps women grow and acquire their rightful dignity and place in society. This ministry has been established in the U.S. and Canada over the past decade largely by devoted women. Sr. Paula Ripple did most of the original groundwork in establishing the North American Conference of Separated and Divorced Catholics organization. Yet I gently suggest to women leaders that they tone down the feminist language at group meetings or all the divorced men will head for the hills. In time men come to appreciate the women's new point of view and that some of their own personal growth is tied up with it. The emergence of many women leaders with this balanced sensitivity has been central to the present growth of divorce ministry.

Support groups are much more effective when men and women contribute together; the complementary characteristics of the sexes can lead to lively interaction and important insights. By listening to a man share his story, a woman may come to a more compassionate understanding of her own former spouse and herself; the same is true of a man when he hears a woman sharing.

Developing male/female friendships which support the recovery process while not short-circuiting it into premature remarriages takes the attention and help of the whole group. I've met divorced men and women who insist that heavy dating and remarriage are simply out of the question for them, but friends of the same sex and opposite sex are necessary for their emotional well-being.

"The young priest in my parish really gets to me," Julie sighed. "He drives me crazy because he's such a nice guy and does such a nice job in the parish in so many ways, but he did it again last Sunday. I know he's trying to be sensitive to divorced people in the congregation, but he said that Jesus loved the prostitutes, the adulterers, and the divorced! I'm really getting sick of being grouped with the prostitutes and the sinners. I don't think I committed a sin in getting divorced. In fact, the most courageous Christian thing I ever did was get us all out of that deadly marriage."

Women today are becoming very sensitive to the suggestion that they are "shady characters" now that they've divorced— "fallen women," or "women on the make." Unfortunately there are many attitudes in our society, and sadly some in the Church, which reinforce these damaging characterizations. Many women feel that everyone loves the adoring little housewife and cute mother, but once a woman asserts her personal value and insists on being treated like an adult, it generates a lot of hostility and resentment from family, friends, and clergy.

"My aunt was married for forty years to my lovable, alcoholic uncle," Julie told me. "He was a good provider, but he was drunk every weekend. The last five years of his life he had an alcoholic brain disease and was like a child; my aunt had an awful time taking care of him. As the Irish would say, she put in her purgatory on earth. I was really surprised when I got divorced that she was one of the few people in my family who reached out to me. 'I hand it to you,' she said. 'I'm glad you girls don't have to endure today what we had to. We had no way out; there was no help available, no treatment. We simply had to offer it up.' I cried when she said that. She had offered it up, and she was a beautiful lady. God had helped her. But I was so grateful that she didn't think I should do the same thing. You see, my husband was alcoholic too."

The fact that we have more divorce today doesn't necessarily mean that we have more bad marriages. It may well be that today people aren't locked into bad marriages in the way they once were. For the first time most women are able to make decisions to end bad marriages. Up until the 1960's, by and large, women simply had to make the best of a bad situation; divorce was unthinkable. In recent years, because of education, economic independence, and changing social, legal, and religious attitudes, women have been able to take responsibility for their lives and attempt to build a new independent life after divorce for themselves and their children.

About ten years ago I was on a radio call-in show with one of the founding mothers of our Boston divorced Catholics group. We took calls over the air for four hours; her Irish-born mother sat that evening with the kids. When my friend came home after midnight her mother was still up, seated with her arms folded on the sofa.

"Did you like the show, Mom?" she asked.

"Isn't it bad enough you're divorced, without having to tell everyone in Boston!" her mother replied.

Getting divorced does involve telling almost everyone about your problems. The worry about shame and embarrassment keeps many people tied to bad marriages. Going public—admitting one's problems and needs—in many cases takes real courage. Women say in the past that they were taught to bear it all silently and cry into their pillows at night. With the help of the Church, many women today are finding the strength to confront the real life situations and are taking the responsibility to make things better.

"*F*ather, I gave her everything she wanted. I sometimes worked two jobs so that we could have two cars, dance lessons and orthodontists for the kids, and summer vacations. She worked hard too. I thought we were in it together. It wasn't always easy. Then one day she tells me our marriage is empty; we don't communicate; she wants a divorce. I couldn't believe it. No one ever told me I was supposed to communicate." Frank's eyes misted over as he told me about his failed marriage.

Many divorced men like Frank feel on the defensive today, and argue that their former wives came up with expectations they never knew were part of married life. Frank says he tried to be a good husband, but found that the rules had changed. Many social observers support Frank's observation by suggesting today that the role definitions of husband and wife have been undergoing significant change in the past generation, with women taking the lead in reshaping the role of wife and mother. Those changes on one side automatically demand adjustment from the other partner; unfortunately many men have not been able to shift gears, because basic assumptions about what it is to be a man in this society—long-time definitions of masculinity, strength, caring, providing, nurturing—have given slowly to change. A widening gap between male and female expectations in many marriages can create strain which leads to separation and divorce.

A Washington rabbi spoke in one of my seminary courses

several years ago about men and the mid-life crisis. He spoke of
several men he knew who over the past year not only left their
wives and children, but also their jobs as well. "It's as if they
were throwing the whole thing over; they said they'd just had it.
They saw themselves putting out all the time at home and on the
job, and getting nothing in return. Unfortunately they had this
romantic idea of living on a houseboat or becoming beach bums
in Tahiti or wildcatting on the Alaskan pipeline. Most soon re-
gretted what they had done, but they couldn't always pick up the
pieces very easily when the damage was already done. Some are
still drifting 'on the houseboat.' "

Longer life in the Western world has created many new demands on marriage, and one is the so-called "mid-life" crisis.
Early in this century, when most men died in their forties and
fifties, there was no such pressure, but today many men wake
up one day, realize they've been married for twenty years and
may face twenty more years of the same situation, and begin to
panic. Some just take off. This crisis is raising questions about
the way we have raised boys to manhood in this society. Psychiatrist Daniel Levenson in his *Seasons of a Man's Life* charts some
main lines of male development and concludes that most U.S.
men are raised to invest most of their personal resources in
"making it" in life, becoming a financial or career success. A
wife and children are at first part of the package but often sec-
ondary. Men are taught to be strong, to tough it out, not to look
for much emotional reward or feedback. Even though they may
have married at an ordinary age, they are raised to postpone their
intimacy needs and "give it all they've got" in order to make their
mark.

In the past many young wives were taught by their mothers
that they'd simply have to put up for a time with his absence or
neglect. That's changed today—young women expect more immediate emotional return in a relationship, and they often want
time for their own careers as well. As traditional standards and

patterns of success for men are questioned, men are influenced by contemporary messages which insist "Do your own thing," "Take care of Number One," "You only go around once," "Catch up on the fun you're missing." The angers and tensions and distress at this difficult time of transition seem to blow many marriages apart before the partners have a chance to pause and get a handle on what is going on. The divorce papers are already in hand before a man sometimes begins to realize that all this was an "expectable" life transition.

In 1975 at the Paulist Center two young male psychologists, one of them divorced, the other happily married, offered an eight week seminar for divorced men on "the male revolution." Some fifteen men met for eight weeks and then agreed to continue meeting for another ten. A number of researchers have told me that the group was most unusual, because it is very hard to get men together and keep them together exploring sensitive issues of male emotional development. These Boston men were committed and worked hard. (It may have been because they knew one another from the larger divorce group and were not strangers, and thus had the security to stay with the group.) Together they talked about maleness and "macho" and the way boys are taught not to cry, not to betray feelings, not to look weak, to answer threat with force. They talked about rigid patterns of male sexual domination, a fear of tenderness, and a fear of women who were too sexually responsive. They talked about their inability to draw out of relationships the kind of sharing and intimacy they hungered for. They talked about homophobia—they fear that "soft" and "tender" men were all gay.

I didn't participate in the group, but joined them for a meeting at the end on their relationship to God. I was surprised at the connections they were beginning to make. Some were beginning to see that their relationship with God was likewise rigid and low on affective content. Just as they hid from any sign of weakness or vulnerability in their relationships with women,

they had a hard time admitting their need for God; they had a
hard time praying. Religion for some of them was always keeping
divine rules and getting a reward. As they began to loosen up
personally with each other, they began to feel more at ease with
me as a priest, and they told of how they began to feel more at
ease with God and began to encounter him in a new way.

My heart went out to these men. I was impressed by their
honesty and straightforwardness, and I was impressed more so
by the concern for one another that surfaced among them, something far more human and expressive than the usual locker-room
banter. They were coming to know themselves for the first time,
coming to know male friends for the first time, and coming to
know their God for the first time.

Men remarry more quickly in this society for several obvious reasons. First of all, there are many more women than
men available for marriage in the society. (If you take out of the
pool of supposedly eligible men those who have died in war, are
in prison, are homosexual, or are functionally retarded, there
are simply not enough available men for all the women currently
looking for husbands.) Since women usually marry men several
years older than themselves, and today often insist that they find
older men more mature and interesting, you can see that there is
a serious shortfall of never-married men available for the never-
married women. This leads many women who have never been
married to consider marrying divorced men, something which
would have been unthinkable for them a generation ago. Men
are also freer to remarry because in 90% of the cases they do not
have custody of children, and in most divorce settlements, because of their earning power, they come out financially ahead.
There is also some evidence that men once married have a
harder time adjusting to a single life alone.

One day a handsome, middle aged man came in to see me,
sat down in my office, and before he could say much began to
cry. The tears streamed down his face, and he looked very em-

barrassed. "I apologize for being such a mess, Father. I'm almost
ashamed to tell you why I'm crying . . . but I moved out of my
house this morning and took a small apartment in the student
area of the city. The apartment is so bare with its plastic rented
furniture. I loved my home; I guess it was really my castle. I had
put a lot of work into it, and had it just the way I wanted it. It's
only been four hours and already I miss my kids. What am I supposed to do now? I really feel lost."

It's been my observation that many divorcing men move
quickly toward new relationships and marriage, not just because
of loneliness, but because their whole life system has collapsed.
There's nothing that defines one's life more than being married;
married couples build a family life together, a social life together, a church life together, a recreational life together. Suddenly that's all gone. "I felt so foolish beginning to date again at
42," Frank told me. "I didn't know how to date anymore and got
nervous about whether I was supposed to pick up the tab or take
the initiative sexually. One woman told me I was a Puritan and
living in the past." Many men seem to move toward remarriage
quickly if they find someone suitable in order to fit in again, have
some companionship, and legitimize their sexual needs. Men
need special support to help them give themselves the necessary
time to absorb and grow through the effects of a failed marriage.
Support groups are vital here.

Mel Krantzler, the author of *Creative Divorce*, once told me
that when he was offering divorce adjustment groups, he would
typically meet men and women recently separated who would
insist that you don't have to be married to be somebody, and they
would go on at length about all the advantages of being single.
But then a prospective new spouse would enter their lives, and
before you could blink, they were talking marriage. The pressure to be coupled, to belong, to fit in, to have a partner, is enormously strong in this society, and men, because they are freer

after divorce, more quickly can take advantage of that pull to marry again.

I have been in several discussions with divorced people about what it takes to be a "real" man or a "real" woman. Once we get beyond the considerations of physical appearance, money, success, sexual power, and prestige, we usually begin to talk about sensitivity, trust, caring qualities, loyalty, warmth and humor. These are qualities that don't come with being male or female, married or single. They come from within, and they need to be nurtured whatever one's life situation. That may be the great discovery for many divorcing men—to learn that they have value in themselves and that value must be developed in them; no one else can put it there for them. Divorce ministry helps many hurting men recover and find that kind of strength in themselves. As Frank put it, "Father, this whole experience has bent me all out of shape emotionally, but I'm beginning to see that it's the best shape I've ever been in. I know I have to put off the thought of remarriage and take care of myself by giving myself more time."

Children

Divorced people worry a lot about their children. The newspapers and magazines are full of reports on the hazards facing children growing up in single parent households. Everywhere divorced Catholics gather, they ask for help in understanding the special needs of their children and advice on how to raise them alone. Non-custodial parents worry too about sustaining good relationships with children they see irregularly. Increasingly children themselves, especially teenagers, ask for help in understanding and supporting their parents.

The first group of divorced people that we gathered in Boston in 1972 listed "helping our kids" as one of their four major goals. We did a number of things to help. We had eight week seminars led by professionals on single parenting, and had special "kids' feasts" at which we gathered the children together for long evenings of eating, sharing and playing games. As we went along we discovered increasingly that the best thing we could do for children was to help their parents. The more we could help a divorcing mother or father work through her or his own adjustment problems, the more it seemed we were doing for the children. Many observers insist that kids often handle the divorce adjustment process about as well as their parents. If the parents are totally upended by the pain of the situation and the household comes apart, the kids are upset too. If the custodial parent provides a good model of coping and carrying on effectively, the kids do well too. If the separated parents can work out a good continuing relationship which keeps the kids from getting caught in the crossfire, the kids will gain.

We learned that all we did to help parents recover personally, psychologically and spiritually profited the children as well. This is not to say that some children did not show signs of extreme and continuing upset, but where the custodial parent was beginning to feel better about herself or himself, the parent was able to help the child work through his own upset. We found that parents, who got involved in support groups, did a better job parenting alone. Raising kids alone is one of the most worrisome and stressful challenges that face the recently separated person; new single parents often feel completely adrift in handling all these practical responsibilities. "Overload" often characterizes their new situation; there just seems to be more and more to do alone, and less and less psychic energy to bring to the tasks. Having to decide things alone, losing the person who knew how to use screwdrivers, and trying to work and help with homework seems at times to be overwhelming. Investing precious time in building a new support network may be the most important investment a custodial single parent makes, since new single parent friends bring much experience and practical wisdom with them.

Support groups also can provide important help for non-custodial parents. Since most non-custodial parents are men, they face the awkward situation of spending large chunks of time visiting with their children where before their time with children was spent in much shorter spans. "You can only go to the zoo and the amusement park and the mall so often on visiting day before it becomes a real drag," Phil told me. Some groups have provided Sunday socials such as picnics and barbecues to which men are invited to bring their children who are with them for the day. Learning to turn visiting time into "quality" time is a real challenge for non-custodial parents. Those seem most fortunate who are able to spend visiting time with the children at their home, allowing the custodial parent some time off and some time to get away.

Despite all the magazine and newspaper articles about the children of divorce, we don't know as much about them as we need to. We simply haven't been able to follow enough of them into adult life to know adequately the long-term consequences of parental divorce. We do know that the effects of divorce are age-related in children; they respond differently to parental separation according to their present developmental stage. Six year olds and fifteen years olds are affected very differently by divorce. The six year old loses a protector, a playmate, a comforter when things go wrong; a fifteen year old loses a role model, someone who knows something about the adult world, someone who provides security at an anxious time of life. Both need attention, but different kids need it given in different ways. It is clear that the departure of one parent, in most cases the father, alters the whole fabric of the child's world and it is never the same again— never quite so good again. That's why children almost always want their parents to get back together again.

Most children at the time of separation show immediate upset, but within six months have resumed their normal lives with friends, school and church. (If children show continuing signs of stress long after this amount of time a school adjustment counselor or some other helping professional should be consulted.) Some children seem to mature more quickly than their peers because of the divorce, and become impressive young people; others seem troubled for many years. There was a myth in American society some decades ago that if parents divorced, their children would turn out to be juvenile delinquents; about a decade ago, we replaced that myth with another myth which said it's better for the kids if troubled parents get a divorce. The truth probably lies somewhere in the middle. Some children pick up and lead well-rounded, healthy lives after parental divorce, while others seem haunted by the sadness of the breakup for years to come. Many juvenile delinquents come from homes where their parents have good marriages; many excellent kids come from homes where their parents have very unsuccessful troubled marriages. In the end, much comes down to the child herself or himself, his or her own emotional resources, the breaks each one gets, and the significant people that enrich their lives after the trauma of divorce.

I read an analysis recently about the incredible popularity of the motion picture "E.T." which spoke especially to divorced kids. In the film a gang of virtuous kids outwit some insensitive adults in order to save their extra-terrestrial visitor, and are assisted in the process by supernatural powers. These children are led by Elliott, a kid who feels alone because his parents have separated but who fearlessly dares to do what is right. Dr. Richard Sloves, a child psychiatrist, says that the message that fairy tales like "E.T." convey to children is that "a struggle against severe difficulties in life is unavoidable, is an intrinsic part of human existence—but that if one does not shy away, but steadfastly meets unexpected and often unjust hardships, one masters all obstacles and at the end emerges victorious." Dr. Sloves feels that children, growing up today in increasingly isolated home environments, need fairy tales even more than children in the past. Furthermore, Dr. Elizabeth Thorne, a child psychologist, says that as unattractive as E.T. may be physically, he is totally unaggressive, benevolent, and charming. The film, she says, "awakes all your desire to believe that you can trust—that you can reach out to a strange person in a strange land." One child of divorced parents told Dr. Sloves that Elliott stayed on earth and did not leave with E.T. at the end because "Elliott has to grow up and you can't grow up on Jupiter; there you stay small and a kid like E.T." Dr. Bruno Bettleheim, speaking of the role of fairy tales in children's lives, writes, "It is, in the final analysis, love which transforms even ugly things into something beautiful."

Nurturing the religious imagination too is an important way of helping children work through the trauma of divorce. When parents become disaffected from the Church at the time of separation, usually children become disconnected as well, and this is a serious loss for them. The truths that so appeal to children in a story like "E.T." are the same truths that give all human life meaning, truths which religion celebrates. Some observers have seen great parallels between the E.T. story and the story of Jesus. Just like E.T., Jesus comes to earth from another world, is found in a shed bathed in light, in his ministry his touch heals, the children are drawn to him, and he dies, is reborn, and eventually goes off to another world. He leaves us behind to grow up like Elliott, to face the loneliness and difficulty of our world, but he remains ever with us.

Children are naturally religious, naturally full of wonder, naturally full of questions, naturally have a sense of the sacredness of life. A solid, mature Christian life on a parent's part—one that faces pain and loss and rejection, and carries on with faith, hope and love—can be an enormously important life model for children. Inviting children to pray with them at times when parents appropriately share their needs and hopes can be an enormously important source of peace and strength for children. Going to Mass, serving on the altar, attending religious education classes, participating in parish youth activities—all these may be more important for the children of divorce than for other children. The bedrock constancy of faith and a surrounding community of loving, caring people can be a great anchor for children at this stressful time.

We hear fear expressed daily that the family is falling apart, and that the many children of divorce are a symptom of family decline. I prefer to look at it differently. Families have always known stress—immigration, political upheaval, lack of medical care, death of young parents by disease, and children dying before the fifth year. The family, as Margaret Mead used to like to say, may be the most resilient institution we have. New times bring new stresses, new challenges, new possibilities. For every case that is made that the family is coming undone, another case is made that it is continuing to change; despite all the change people still want lasting marriages and still want to live together with their children in happiness and security. More children live with at least one natural parent in the U.S. today than ever before. We have always had large numbers of children in single-parent families, but in the past more were living with relatives and family friends or in foster homes or orphanages. Everywhere I travel these days I meet many resourceful single parents and resourceful non-custodial parents and their children who are shaping new, loving, successful lives for themselves.

Remarriage

About 75% of Catholics who divorce eventually remarry, with about half of them doing so within three years. The reasons for remarriage are easy to understand: men and women who once decided that marriage was for them usually do not sour on marriage because their first attempt failed; if anything, for many people a failed marriage only makes them yearn all the more for a good marriage. Living alone or raising children alone over many years is not a very attractive prospect for most people. In a highly mobile society where most people live far from their birthplace and do not have supportive networks of family and friends nearby, marriage has become the ordinary pathway to companionship, intimacy and personal fulfillment for the overwhelming majority of people. (About 90% of Americans marry in their lifetimes, a greater percentage than at any time in our history.) The majority of Catholics divorce before they are 35, which gives both men and women a normal life expectancy of 35–40 more years of life after divorce. Not remarrying, and living alone all that time, is a burdensome prospect for most.

Many divorced people do not have the option to remarry, especially women raising children alone since few men want to take on a ready-made family. Others are so wounded by the sad effects of divorce that remarriage seems out of the question for them, at least for the foreseeable future. The Church's ministry to divorced Catholics has as its major goal supporting men and women in developing a viable single life after divorce; whether people eventually remarry or not, single autonomy is seen as an immediate goal for all, since those who can't live alone can't live with another very well. Many first marriages failed because one partner depended too much on another for personal identity, fulfillment and personal happiness, and eventually the marriage collapsed under the burden of unrealistic demands.

I've met many divorced Catholics who said that remarriage was simply out of the question for them after divorce; they needed time to sort out their own personal goals and needs—they could not consider remarrying without the Church's approval. Fortunately, the expanding, compassionate ministry of the Catholic marriage tribunals is providing annulments of more and more failed marriages and providing new marriages with Church blessing for thousands of divorced Catholics. It is hard to determine what percentage of failed marriages can be annulled, but informed estimates suggest anywhere from 25% to 50% of first marriages which end in divorce can be annulled; that's why divorce ministry suggests that divorced Catholics, after some time has passed and they feel reasonably well adjusted to the many problems that follow divorce—even if they have no immediate plans to marry—should consult with an informed Church person about the possibility of annulment.

The enormous amount of personal and financial resources that the Church invests in the work of the marriage tribunals is itself a concrete sign that the Church recognizes the need of second marriage for many people and is trying to provide such new marriages with Church approval. (About 75% of annulments granted come in cases where at least one of the parties to the first marriage is already married again.) In its pastoral concern the Church wants to do all it can to help these second married Catholics live in good standing in the Church community.

At the same time, many Catholics go ahead and remarry without the Church's approval. When they do so, they break a Church law which prohibits such a marriage, and are in what the Church officially terms an "irregular second union." (A regular second union would be one where an annulment has been obtained for any previous marriages.) Such irregularly married Catholics remain part of the Church community; they are not excommunicated from the Church as was once the legal penalty for such an action. (The American law of excommunication for such second marriages was removed in 1977.) In 1981 Pope John Paul II encouraged such second married Catholics to participate in the lives of their parishes, pray, work and serve with their fellow Catholics. He reaffirmed the traditional norm of the Church which holds that such second married Catholics cannot receive the Eucharist, because their new "irregular" second marriages place them at odds with the Church's teaching and laws on marriage. Yet this traditional norm does not rule out Communion for the second married in every case; there may be exceptions in some cases based on a consideration of why the first marriage failed and the Christian commitment of the couple in the new marriage. The second married should always seek to resolve the status of their marriage through the tribunal which provides clear access after annulment to Communion for them; where this is not possible they should talk over their situation with a priest or other Church pastoral minister who can assist them in making an appropriate decision about reception of the Eucharist. There is a great deal of discussion and discernment that goes into this "conscience search" with such a spiritual guide; ultimately the decision to take Communion rests with the individuals themselves. They alone can decide whether there is any barrier that keeps them from receiving the Eucharist in faith and love. Many theologians and pastors argue that where a couple in a second marriage has made a permanent Christian commitment until death in this new marriage, are leading good Christian lives, are raising children in the faith, and are faithful to personal and financial obligations that still obtain from a prior marriage, and where no scandal would be given by their receiving Communion, they should be offered in the Eucharist the spiritual nourishment they need to fulfill the Christian obligations that are theirs in this new marriage. The welcoming of Catholics in second marriages, not approved by the Church, to Communion admits of disagreement at this time in the Church's life. I have usually found that the best place to get the best-informed advice on this issue is by contacting either a priest who is active in divorced Catholics ministry, the marriage tribunal or the family life office of the local diocese.

The Church is becoming increasingly concerned about preparing couples for second marriages, especially when they are entering such marriages with the Church's blessing. We might guess that those who failed once at marriage would be wiser and more cautious the second time around, but government data makes a different case. The U.S. Census Bureau estimates that of all new second marriages entered into this year, 45% of them will eventually end in a second divorce. These are the reasons suggested for the high failure rate in second marriages: (1) the rebounding effect, i.e., people rush into a new marriage as a way of curing the distress brought on by a first divorce, so consequently the second marriage is overburdened by the unfinished emotional agenda remaining from the failed relationship; (2) complicated emotional demands and pressures brought on by blended families, and difficulties in relating to an expanded network of family and new relatives; (3) inadequate skills at communication and negotiation necessary to resolve the complex issues raised by this new marriage. Increased attention in recent years has been focused on the complications raised by stepfamilies. Many couples would like to believe that children will adjust, but this is not necessarily so. Children will only cooperate in a new family situation if they feel respected, consulted and included. Complex authority, financial and life-style issues involving children can create grave tensions. Even relating to stepchildren in non-custodial situations may be extremely demanding; such children may not like a new stepparent at all, and make it quite clear that they don't. Disapproving family members and relatives may be ignored initially, but in time such alienation can become burdensome, especially at holidays or at times of sickness or death.

Newly developed second marriage preparation programs are helping couples think through the following questions: (1) How does this new marriage affect us religiously, especially our traditional values and our place in the Church community? (2) How is this new marriage going to be different from both our former marriages? What have we learned? If one partner has never been married does he/she understand how the divorce affected his/her fiancé/fiancée and how he/she has dealt with it? (3) Have the complex relationships involved in blending families or relating to natural children who will not be living in been thoroughly explored and prepared for? (4) Have next of kin been informed and their support elicited, even if grudgingly? (5) Have the usual issues that face any marrying couple—sexuality, finances, communication, children—been thoroughly discussed and a commitment to ongoing dialogue and negotiation made?

The seventeenth century British historian Samuel Johnson once said that remarriage is always a triumph of hope over experience. I have a psychiatrist friend who says he would never recommend second marriage—it's just too complicated, too chancy, too open to further failure and pain. Whatever the cautions that may be voiced, large numbers of Catholic divorced men and women, people who consider themselves good Catholics, who love their Church and want to remain part of it, are making decisions to marry again even though the Church does not approve of such marriages. They respect the teaching of Jesus and the Church that marriage should be permanent, lasting until death; many will say they wish they had had just such a marriage. They are not promoting divorce and remarriage—they wish they did not have to go through all this upset, and would never wish it on anyone else. Yet they have become convinced that their human well-being and their Christian well-being will be enhanced if they find a lifelong, loving companion in a new marriage. It pains them that they cannot have the Church's approval for such a step, but they reluctantly go against the Church's discipline, convinced that such a step is bringing them closer to God and ultimately closer to the Church. Their decision, they insist, should not be interpreted as hostility toward the Church or a rejection of its teaching; they find the Church's laws too strict in their particular case. They see their decision to remarry as a very personal decision, made for their own personal well-being; they fully hope in this new marriage to stay close to God and the Church community.

Around the issue of remarriage for divorced Catholics we find the Church community dealing with some very new social and human pressures, and beginning to marshal its traditional resources to help those entering second marriages. It is a difficult issue of change in a turbulent Church at a turbulent time, but we do see the Church beginning to respond today with openness and compassion, struggling to understand and accept the need of so many divorced persons for new marriages.

Believing

Journey

"*I* grew up fully expecting I'd get married some day, have a family, and live happily ever after. There would be a kind of neat progression to it all. Now that I'm divorced, I feel as though I've fallen off the track, and I wonder if I'll ever be able to get back on. There weren't supposed to be all these bumps and detours. I wonder if I'll ever be able to straighten my life out."

Ray, a construction worker, shared his dilemma with me at a workshop group in Mississippi. He touched a common anxiety and common perception that seems to disturb many divorced people.

Maybe deep within all of us there is a need to have a neatly ordered life, where everything falls into place, and where there are no surprises which knock us off our feet. There's a way of looking at life which sees all of us in this world moving along a straight and narrow road; if everyone stays on the path and behaves as he or she is supposed to, he or she will find happiness. If he or she gets off the road, gets lost or loses the map or sets off in another direction, he or she is inviting chaos and suffering. In this way of looking at things, a divorce is one of those events which destroys the plan, messes up the journey, and brings certain distress. The orderly plan is God's plan for us and all human beings. Divorce isn't in his plan—those who divorce are bringing their own suffering on themselves.

"You may not have thought about life in quite those terms," I told the Mississippi divorced Catholics, "but the more you

79

think about it, the more you may discern that a lot of the distress that follows broken marriages for many of you comes from just such a deep-seated conviction that you have veered off the right path in life and are headed now in the wrong direction. Furthermore, now that a divorce has been finalized, there doesn't seem to be any way to get back on the safe course. Things just seem permanently messed up."

I proposed to them another way of looking at life—one that is more fundamentally Christian, and one that helps us deal better with the many mishaps in life such as divorce. It invites us to look upon life as a journey to the Kingdom of God; the destination is the same for everyone, but there are many different maps and many different routes. Some resourceful people seem to move along the journey to the Father with great ease and facility; others seem to lose their way from time to time, and some really get lost. Some insist on branching out on their own and charting their own course. As strange as it may seem, for those who get lost now and then or those who get there by a circuitous route, the getting there becomes all the more joyful. The good shepherd left the ninety-nine behind to find the lost sheep and carried him home on his shoulders.

Jim and Evelyn Whitehead in their book *Marrying Well* suggest that looking at marriage as a journey is deeply rooted in the Jewish/Christian tradition. "It reminds us of the perils and revelations to be experienced along the way. It recalls tests of faith and celebrates—in burning bushes and manna in the desert—the signs that God is still with us." They remind us that up until recently in the Catholic community marriage was seen as an institution or a state of life. Catholics could expect to live in such a "state" with confidence and clarity of purpose, with doctrinal and moral rules that seemed clear and consistent. Family, Church and society safeguarded these rules. Living by the rules and staying on the straight and narrow road would bring happiness here and hereafter. For some Christians it always will.

Yet we see in the Old Testament that God taught and shaped the Israelite people into his own people by testing them and challenging them throughout an unpredictable journey in the desert. All the fear and uncertainty, the threat and the confusion of that long desert march became the way God instructed and toughened this people. The many hazards of the journey drew them closer to him and closer to each other. In the New Testament, the Gospel writers use journey as a way of describing Jesus' public ministry. On his final journey up to Jerusalem, Jesus is drawn even closer to his Father, drawn closer to God's suffering people, drawn deeper into conflict with those who resisted his mission. Jesus' journey prepares him for the final gift of himself on Good Friday; it is a demanding, unsettling, threatening road.

Christian literature through the centuries is full of Canterbury pilgrims and missionaries leaving their homelands to sacrifice all for Christ. At the Second Vatican Council when the bishops of the world searched for new language to describe the Church, they drew upon some very old biblical language and described the Church today as a pilgrim people on a journey to the Kingdom of God. We have no homeland, no secure possessions, no perfect maps; we are drawn through time and history over unfamiliar terrain to God's home; we are challenged to invite others to join us on this exposed, perilous trip, promising them only the hardship of travel but ultimately a great heavenly feast.

A pilgrim people on a journey seems to be a much more helpful way of describing us as a Christian people in today's world. We know where we're going, but we're not always sure these days how we are going to get there. We feel that we are less a people in secure possession of God and more a people in pursuit of God's sometimes shadowy but no less real presence in our lives. We struggle daily to be faithful to a God whose call to us is not always clear; we strain to perceive the modern equivalents of "the cloud by day and the pillar of fire by night." We seem to need new resources of reconciliation and maturity if we are to manage the stresses of the journey and persevere. We find ourselves forced to travel light, sometimes without the easy answers of childhood religious beliefs, or sometimes without the warm support of family and friends close at hand, or even without a spouse who meets our expectations of what a husband or wife is supposed to be. Fatigue is a constant companion on such a difficult journey, and one faces the terror of losing one's way— even one's partner—to forces and events beyond one's control. It seems at times that the more we travel, the more the road winds unexpectedly and the less clear our destination becomes. Our burdens seem heavier and resources become more limited; we sense an ebbing of youthful enthusiasms and energy and seem to face daily the drudgery of the road. We find some companions who support us on the way and we lose others—we yearn for God to lead us and replenish our fidelity and patience and strength.

The Lord did not promise us a detailed road map but only a destination and some principles to guide us on our journey. He makes us fill in the details ourselves and shape our own path. He is with us always, but it is truly our journey, and the getting there is worked out by our own trial and error. He doesn't lead us by hand, but gives us a hand on our way. He did not promise us that our journey through life would be, unlike his, free of doubts and depressions and dry spells. What he did promise is that he would help us along the way build a deeper, ever newer life by confronting our weakness, our brokenness, our need for him, and he promised that he would help us grow throughout trials and failures and even our tragic breakups.

The psychologist Erik Erikson once wrote: "I shall present human growth from the point of view of the conflicts, inner and outer, which the vital personality weathers, re-emerging from each crisis with an increased sense of inner unity, with an increase of good judgment, and an increase of the capacity "to do well" according to his own standards and the standards of those who are significant to him." Our Christian faith is an important meaning system that helps make sense of the turbulence which comes into one's life. The religious metaphor of journey is a powerful way of including life tragedies such as divorce in the ongoing fabric of one's life, rather than seeing divorce as something which never fits. Journeying and being a pilgrim people is not easy. No traveler pulls it all off perfectly; everyone gets lost or discouraged from time to time. The challenge is to pick oneself up, recommit oneself to the journey, find new companions, and go on.

I presented this different Christian worldview to my divorced friends in Mississippi and was struck by their response. One divorced and remarried man, a store owner in his late fifties, told me that this way of looking at things had never occurred to him before. "I had all that fine Jesuit education," he said, "which placed me square on the straight and narrow; when my marriage of thirty years came apart, and when five years later I chose to remarry, I felt I had simply blown the whole system. There was no way, it seemed to me, I could get back on the right path. Now I can see there are many different paths with many setbacks, and many challenges to begin again; but God stays with us through it all, leading us home. I do feel that I have become a better person through what has happened to me. My getting divorced and risking commitment in a new marriage has made me a more compassionate person. I used to be as self-righteous as the next guy; now I think I'm a bit more sympathetic to others. I think I'll go much farther with these new attitudes than I ever would have gone with the old way of looking at things."

The journey metaphor doesn't suggest that broken marriage and tragedy must come to every life. What it does mean is that every life, even those of couples in lasting first marriages, will experience stress, falling out, and the need for recommitment and renewed perseverance. For those whose life maps lead to a dead end, where one's companions prove inadequate for the demands of the trail, and where one has to renegotiate one's life pattern, this can be a time for growth, rededication and deepened resources. Whatever happens to us can fit into the journey as long as we do not give up and do not abandon the search for the Kingdom of God. The faithful search for God's love and peace may lead us down many difficult roads with many unlikely companions on a journey we never imagined or even wanted, but the Lord promises that if we persevere in faith he will be there at journey's end.

Gifts

*L*ast year a man named Sal told me at a conference in Miami: "Father, you said something at a talk here several years ago, which I've never forgotten. In fact, it changed my life!"

My ears perked up, and I asked: "What did I say?"

"You said divorce could be a gift! At first I thought that was a crazy idea, but you know what—three years later I'm beginning to appreciate what you were talking about!"

I've spoken about the possibility of divorce being a gift a number of times, and I have always been struck by the response it generates, positive and negative.

Some people sit there with puzzled looks on their faces. I can almost hear them saying to themselves, "How could anything this terrible which has caused me so much pain and upset, which has left my life a mess, be a gift? If this is what you call a gift, you can keep it. No thanks."

Others who have gained some distance on their failed marriage and have grown and changed look at me more openly. They're beginning to realize that they could never return to the marriage. So much has happened, so much has been gained—they're different persons. In fact they've begun to discover resources and skills in themselves they never knew were there. They've begun to realize that they were tied into a deadening situation which was hurting them and their former spouse. They may never have looked upon the experience as a gift, but I can tell they're thinking to themselves: "Maybe he's got a point."

Then there are those, like Sal in Miami, who know exactly what I'm talking about. They're new people. They have no desire to go back where they were, and they know they couldn't go back to where they were. Not that the whole divorce experience was all sweetness and light. Not that getting a divorce was a nifty way to grow. Not that they're recommending it to others. But for them this sad, tragic experience has become the passageway to a new life, and they're now grateful.

When Jesus meets the divorced Samaritan woman at Jacob's well in the Gospel of John (Chapter 4), he says to her, "If only you recognized God's gift, and who it is that is speaking with you . . . ." Divorce is a tangled, sorrow-filled experience, one of the most stressful human experiences anyone can go through. I certainly don't recommend it as a way to grow. Yet when this tangle of emotions, personal history, and personal limits is confronted with faith and hope and love, it can become the source of a whole new way of living. We Christians believe that God speaks to us in many ways, and I like to suggest that he even speaks to us through the experience of divorce.

> But looking up he saw the rich who were putting their gifts into the treasury. And he saw also a certain poor widow putting in two small coins. And he said, "Truly I say to you, this poor widow has put in more than all. For all these, out of their abundance, have put in gifts to God; but she out of her want has put in all that she had to live on."

That beautiful Gospel story tells me something about divorce as a gift. We can see Jesus with his disciples sitting near the temple treasury and noticing the people coming and going, placing their offerings in the box. A number of well-dressed men and women come by and noisily drop in their coins with great show. They already have their reward. Then along comes a poor widow in black, moving quietly to avoid notice, and she drops in two little coins which make hardly a sound. Think of the poverty of her gift, yet the richness of her offering. Jesus points out that she gave much more than those who put gold in the treasury.

That's the kind of gift divorce can be. It's a poor gift—so much sadness, so much pain, so much heartbreak. It brings a time of extreme want. One feels empty, without resources; nothing in life seems to have any value. Yet when we give this experience to God, it becomes like gold. For the Lord gives back to us all we need to find in this difficult experience—insight, personal resources, courage. I don't wish to glamorize the divorce experience. That's why I like the Gospel story of the widow so much. The threads of the divorce experience are not golden; its threads often tell of human frailty, poor judgment, self-inflicted injury. But when these poor, human dramas are given to the Lord, he transforms them into gold.

About fifteen years ago when I was a very young priest, I studied marriage counseling in Chicago and worked for the marriage counseling agency of the archdiocese. My specialty was short-term counseling for young couples who were having expected adjustment problems. A wonderful psychiatrist, who was our teacher and consultant at the agency, had all the staff to his home one evening for a party. I was walking about admiring the art on his apartment walls when I came across a striking carving of Jesus after the scourging. It was only about nine inches high, but the artist had powerfully captured the overwhelming sadness in Jesus' face. When I told my psychiatrist friend how much I was struck by the carving, he said, "Take it." I looked at him with an amazed grin and said: "Take it?"

"Sure, if you like it, I'd like you to have it. You only possess a work of art if you give it away."

My psychiatrist friend captured for me one of the most

striking paradoxes of human experience: we only possess a gift if
we give it away.

> These twelve Jesus sent forth, having instructed them
> in this way: Go to the lost sheep of the house of Israel.
> And as you go preach the message: "The Kingdom of
> God is at hand!" Cure the sick, raise the dead, cleanse
> the lepers, cast out devils. The gift you have received,
> give as a gift (Mt 10:8).

Divorce, as a gift, is not something to be hoarded and kept
under a bushel measure. If it's just my personal growth, my special experience, it will remain brittle and frail. There is no real
lasting growth, no real lasting change, unless we begin to share
what we have been given, what we have learned. The real gift-
edness of the experience begins to deepen as we reach out to help
others. "The gift you have received, give as a gift." This is the
essential dynamic of divorce support groups where men and
women who have gained from their experience and put together
a new life reach out to support and heal others who are newly
caught in the trauma and see no way out for themselves. As truly
as the Lord sent out the twelve to preach, cure the sick, raise the
dead, and cleanse the lepers, so does he send believing divorced
men and women out to bring his healing love to others who are
knotted in conflict and misery. What these divorce ministers
bring is the gift they have received, and in sharing their experience they own it all the more. They gain newer insight and
greater strength by reaching out to the newly hurting. In giving
away the gift, they truly possess it.

> There are different kinds of spiritual gifts, but the
> same Spirit gives them. There are different ways of
> serving, but the same Lord is served. There are differ-
> ent abilities to perform service, but the same God gives

ability to everyone for their particular service. The
Spirit's presence is shown in some way in each person
for the good of all (1 Cor 12:4–8).

When I was a boy of nine I came across what I thought was
the greatest story ever written. The reason was quite simple: the
hero of this story was named Jim Young. I'm sure you can imagine a child's elation to find a fictional character bearing his
name. The story was O. Henry's "The Gift of the Magi."

We all remember the young husband and wife in turn-of-
the-century New York who were too poor to buy Christmas presents for each other. Jim pawns his most treasured possession,
his grandfather's gold watch, to buy his wife some silver combs
for her shiny long brown hair. Della sells her cascading brown
hair to buy Jim a platinum fob chain for his watch. They laughed
and cried on Christmas Eve when they realized how they had
sacrificed for each other. O. Henry concludes his tale:

The magi, as you know, were wise men—wonderfully
wise men—who brought gifts to the Babe in the man-
ger. They invented the art of giving Christmas presents. Being wise, their gifts were no doubt wise ones,
possibly bearing the privilege of exchange in case of
duplication. And here I have lamely related to you the
uneventful chronicle of two foolish children in a flat
who most unwisely sacrificed for each other the greatest treasures of their house. But in a last word to the
wise of these days let it be said that of all who give gifts
these two were the wisest. Of all who give and receive
gifts, such as they are the wisest. Everywhere they are
the wisest. They are the magi.

These two were the wisest because they sacrificed their
most treasured possessions for each other, yet they received a

much richer gift in return—mutual love. Their gifts were so poor, but their offering was so rich. They gave away what they possessed, and possessed each other all the more. O. Henry portrayed in his little tale a truth as old as the Gospel. Only when we give ourselves away do we really possess our lives and each other. Only when we reach out in love and service to others do we learn that we are loved. "It's in giving that we receive, and in dying that we are born to life."

The Midwest Medical Mission is a group of doctors, medical technicians, nurses and other medical personnel who go each year for a month to Haiti to bring medical healing to the poorest people of that poorest nation in this hemisphere. CBS "Sunday Morning" went along with the group some months ago and showed their makeshift hospital in the jungle and the hundreds of people who had walked miles to get help. The doctors performed corrective surgery on cleft palates, goiters, and broken limbs. The TV show filmed a remarkable scene of an old man thanking and praising the doctors because they had saved his daughter's life. The TV interviewer asked the physician who heads the medical team why they come to Haiti each year.

"I'm a Christian," the doctor said, "who takes quite seriously the words of Jesus: 'From those to whom much has been given, much will be expected.' And yet I don't want to give the impression of a kind of stoical determination that brings us here to Haiti. We receive far more from these good people than we bring to them. I am continually touched by their devotion to each other, their courage in the face of overwhelming pain, their warm gratitude."

. . . though we are many, we are one body in union with Christ, and we are all joined to each other as different parts of one body. So we are to use our different gifts in accordance with the grace God has given us. If our gift is to speak God's message, we should do it according to the faith that we have; if it is to serve, we should serve; if it is to teach, we should teach; if it is to encourage others, we should do so . . . . Love one another warmly as Christian brothers and sisters, and be eager to show respect for one another. Work hard and do not be lazy. Serve the Lord with a heart full of devotion. Let your hope keep you joyful, be patient in your troubles, and pray at all times. Share your belongings with your needy fellow Christians, and open your homes to strangers. Be happy with those who are happy, weep with those who weep. Have the same concern for everyone. (Rom 12:4–18).

Sal from Miami and many, many other divorced Catholics are learning that divorce can be a gift. They are recognizing it, giving it away, and becoming new men and women in the process.

God

"*I* couldn't figure out why God was letting this happen to me." Caroline was almost in tears as she spoke. "What had I ever done wrong? I'd always been a good Catholic. Why did God seem to abandon me in all this hurt and pain? Where is God now when I need him?"

We talked about the fact that any severe human crisis can create a crisis in our relationship with God. After sharing for a while, I asked her to think for a moment or two about her image or picture of God. "What image comes into your mind? How do you usually imagine God?" I asked. We decided that for most of us those warm, loving images of God we learned as a child come flashing across the screens of our minds when we tried to picture God. The picture may not quite be the old man with the long white beard sitting on a platinum throne in the clouds, but that's close. Caroline said that when she thinks of God she often sees Jesus with a warm smile, reaching out to her and embracing her. Other times she thinks of the Sacred Heart or recalls the warm closeness that she experiences after receiving Holy Communion. Most of the time she sees God as her friend.

"Did you ever think of God as a wrestler?" I asked. She looked at me blankly. I explained that I never did until recently when a friend, Jim Whitehead, pointed out a marvelous passage in the Old Testament in which God reveals himself as a wrestler. It's part of the familiar story of Jacob and Esau. We remember from our Bible history classes that Jacob and Esau were the sons of Isaac and Rachel. Esau was the elder son, Jacob the younger. Rachel favored Jacob, and suggested that he go in to his old, blind father, pose as his brother Esau, and get his father's special blessing, the blessing reserved to the first-born. Jacob deceived his father and received the blessing. When his brother learned that he had been cheated, he turned on Jacob in anger. Jacob then fled from the wrath of his brother and settled far away in the land of Laban, marrying and raising a large, wealthy family.

Many years later Jacob was filled with sorrow at the continuing alienation he experienced from his brother. So he decided to journey to see Esau, and to try to make peace. He didn't know how he'd be received—whether Esau would attack him and his family or welcome him. As he neared the land of Esau, he sent messengers ahead with gifts for Esau; he then made camp for the night, waiting for word. I got out my Bible and read to Caroline from the Book of Genesis:

> So the gifts went ahead of Jacob while he lodged that night in the camp. That same night he arose, took his two wives, the two maids, and his eleven sons, and forded the river Jaboc. He took them and sent them across the stream, with everything that belonged to him; but Jacob himself remained behind, all alone. Someone wrestled with him until the break of dawn. When the wrestler saw that he could not overcome Jacob, he touched the socket of Jacob's thigh so that it was dislocated while Jacob wrestled with him. Then the wrestler said, "Let me go; it is dawn." But Jacob answered, "I will not let you go until you bless me." Then he asked Jacob, "What is your name?" And he answered, "Jacob." He said, "You shall no longer be called Jacob, but Israel, because you have contended with God and men, and have triumphed." Jacob asked,

"What is your name?" He answered, "Why do you ask my name?" The wrestler blessed him there. Jacob named the place Phanuel, saying, "I have seen a heavenly being face to face, yet my life has been spared" (Gen 32:22–31).

Caroline and I admitted that we never wrestled as a sport, but we both had memories of wrestling with brothers and sisters or friends when growing up. Caroline remembered being told all the time that girls weren't supposed to be so rough. There can be a wonderful closeness to wrestling, we agreed, a way of expressing playful intimacy and fondness for one another. Yet wrestling can also be dangerous; necks can get twisted and arms bruised. At the heart of wrestling there's ambiguity—real closeness requires risk.

It may be hard, I went on, for us at first to think of God as someone who wrestles with us, but this may be an excellent image for describing the relationship with God which many divorced people experience. God comes close to us during the heartbreak and agony of divorce. I've heard many people say that they never felt closer to God than at this time. Yet God also seems to put divorcing persons to the test at this time, literally knocking them upside down, off their pins, twisting and shaking every aspect of their life.

God wrestles with us as a way of coming close to us and helping us grow. If you've ever observed young high school wrestlers, you can see that all the intense physical activity builds up their muscles. Wrestling with God during the divorce transition can be a way of growing stronger while one is tremendously upset. Jacob held onto the mysterious wrestler through the night. He might have given in or he might have fled from the wrestler's embrace. Rather he held his own. How often is the divorcing person tempted to give in—to wallow in self-pity, to escape into martinis or tranquilizers, or just drop out. How often is the di-

vorcing person tempted to flee—to leave everyone and everything and just take off, flee into a new relationship which will
make everything instantly better. Rather, God who wrestles
with us invites us to hang onto the uncertainty of the recovery
process—to hold onto one's values and one's faith amid the stress
and strain, and to be confident one is gaining strength.

After the long struggle, the wrestling God wounds Jacob.
We read later in the same chapter from Genesis that Jacob limps
away from the scene with the socket of his thigh dislocated. Divorce is a permanent wounding. In a very real way, a broken
marriage relationship never goes away. There's a kind of permanent injury that divorced persons carry always—not an injury
that leaves them sad and dejected all the time, but an injury that
keeps them in touch with a most significant life experience.
There's an obvious temptation in the midst of all the pain and
upset to try to blot the past out. Caroline tried to say to herself:
"This divorce wasn't so bad. It really didn't hurt very much. I'm
better than ever. It's as if I were never married."

The key, we agreed, is what we do with the wounding.
What does it say about us? What does it say about a God who lets
us be wounded? A God who protected us from all human adversity and pain would be a God who treated us like fragile children.
Our God, the wrestler of Genesis, is a God who calls us to become men and women, strong, resourceful, independent. He invites us to see during this difficult time that the only pathway to
human maturity is through suffering and pain, that like broken
bones that heal, we can grow stronger in the broken places. Isn't
that the model of human growth he has shown us in his only
Son, who passed through rejection and death to new life? The
great potential of the divorce transition is that God comes very
close to us, and he reveals himself to us—not as the smiling old
man with the white beard who overprotects, or the warm Jesus
who makes us happy, but rather as a God who turns us upside
down and invites us to get up as stronger, wiser people.

Every failed marriage was in some way a prison which confined and restricted. There may have been much Christian gain in working through the many tensions and problems of that marriage, but now that it is over, God offers another opportunity to come closer to him and to come closer to ourselves. The closeness to him comes from entering into the long nighttime struggle of gaining self-knowledge, understanding the past, grasping a good sense of one's resources, developing a new vision of what one can become. Our God shakes us, knocks us off our pins, takes us to the mat, all the while inviting us to grow stronger and closer to him. He wrestles with us because he loves us, not in a smothering, overprotective way, but with a love that strains to set us free.

Jacob limped away and became the father of a great people. A divorced person gingerly moves beyond the experience and can become a better Christian. Our wounds remind us of the struggle, and in the Christian scheme of things they teach us humility and draw us closer to others who are wounded. St. Paul brags about his woundedness over and over in his letters; he says that when he was truly weak but held on, he discovered the power of God in his life. From holding on despite his weakness he was able to say, "I can do all things in him who strengthens me." Our woundedness can make us stronger yet more vulnerable, tougher but more open, rock-like yet more compassionate.

The gift of having wrestled with God and having been wounded is that we develop a radar for others who are suffering. We find ourselves drawn to those who are hurting, not pitying them but inviting them to enter the struggle. I've seen this happen so often in divorce sharing groups where those who are further along reach out tenderly to the recently separated, gently shaking them up by posing the tough questions and calling them out of their own misery.

The God who comes close to us as a wrestler during the divorce transition teaches us an important lifelong lesson about closeness and intimacy. That closeness in human relationships which is comforting and makes one feel better, but has no challenge and no gritty human interaction, is not real intimacy. It is a caricature of intimacy. When adults come close to each other, two growing, changing people who have a real sense of who they are and what they want out of life, the relationship is marked by ambiguity, negotiation, compromise. But here in that tough human interaction, real joyful intimacy is found.

Caroline and I agreed that the divorced friends we know who are living the most together lives as single persons or as remarried Catholics are those who have learned to love a wrestling God and have learned to prize their own personal resourcefulness and maturity. At some point they learned to stand on their own two feet, even with a limp.

I told Caroline that Jim Whitehead says that God in his continuing revelation of himself reveals us to ourselves. He comes close to us so that we can discover who we are; and when we really begin to know ourselves, we come closer to knowing him. He loves it when we wrestle back, when we grapple and challenge and refuse to let go; he loves it when we push back with all our force against him, demanding his blessing. Our God is not out there, above it all, looking down, keeping track, totaling up points. Rather he's a God who's down here with us, wrestling with us in the rough and tumble of human existence, inviting us to come closer to him and closer to one another and ourselves. Caroline told me when leaving that she'd have to do a lot of thinking about God the wrestler.

Jesus

"*I* couldn't figure out why I felt so ugly and so dirty after my divorce," Eileen told me. "I was so self-conscious. I felt that everyone was looking at me and was seeing right through me. I felt that everyone knew all about me, and I felt ashamed. I wanted to hide."

Eileen and I talked a lot about her self-image, and the fact that such loss of self-esteem is a common after-effect of separation and divorce. During one of our conversations I shared with her this poem by Robert W. Castle, Jr., from *Prayers from the Burned-Out City*:

Did you look like that, Lord?
What I mean to say is this:
    I saw a picture of you the other day.
You looked so clean.
Your clothes were so white—so very white.
Your face was so white, too.
All clean and antiseptic.
You looked like you were just dry-cleaned, Lord.
You know—pressed and clean.
And your hair looked like you just had a permanent wave,
    And there you were like a big success.

Did you look like that, Lord?
I always had the feeling you lived out with the
    people in the streets and roads.

I don't imagine you could keep your clothes
    or yourself very clean there.
Your skin must have been naturally dark,
    and burned even more by the sun.

Maybe you had a strong, hooked nose and were going a
        little bald.
Did you look like that, Lord?
I don't know, and it just doesn't make much difference;
    but I'm sure you weren't a white, Irish Catholic!
My prayer to you, Lord,
    is to thank you for being so beautiful a person
    in what you said and how you lived.
That's the real picture of you,
    and the one we all need to see.
Help us see you real, Lord. Amen.

Many of us were raised on the holy-card Jesus, who, as the poem suggests, was all pressed and clean and looked like a big success. After all he was God; he had it all together. We were all taught that he loved us and cared for us and we could turn to him in time of trouble, but he seemed so far removed from our lives. Unfortunately many divorcing people do not see much connection between the holy-card Jesus and themselves at this painful time. They learned as children that Jesus was betrayed, rejected and abandoned, and that he was eventually killed, but they still don't see much connection between what happened to him and their own lives.

I can remember a story where the child Jesus was playing with some other children at Nazareth, and they were all making birds out of mud. The friends of Jesus shaped birds of many different sizes and shapes, but when Jesus finished making his, he would touch them and they would fly away. Somehow when we read the Gospel stories about Jesus suffering, we sometimes

have the sense that, unlike ourselves, he could always touch the
pain and make it go away. He may have gone through all that to
teach us some lessons, but down deep we always had the sense
that it was easier for him because he was God. He never suffered
the way we have!

We Christians have always believed that Jesus was truly
God and truly man. Yet many of us have had difficulty in pin-
ning down exactly what being "truly human" meant. Understanding the true humanity of Jesus is essential if suffering
people, especially the divorced, are to find in Jesus a true
brother in their time of need. The Letter to the Hebrews in the
New Testament says: "He had to be made like his brothers and
sisters in every respect, so that he might become a merciful and
faithful high priest in the service of God" (Heb 2:17). Jesus was
truly a flesh and blood person, with spirit, soul and body like
ours. Like us he thought about friends, like us he planned holi-
day celebrations, like us he laughed at stories and wept at death.
He was emotionally touched by the beauty of lilies in the field or
the soldier who worried about his sick servant. The Letter to the
Hebrews continues: "Because he himself suffered and was
tempted, he is able to help those who are tempted. We do not
have a high priest who is unable to sympathize with our weaknesses, but one who in every respect was tempted as we are, yet
without sin" (Heb 4:14). He smoothed the wood at Nazareth
with his own calloused hands; he meditated often on the prophets in the Hebrew Scriptures; he truly loved his mother, his
friends, his disciples. Like us he grew in wisdom and grace; he
changed, he learned, his feelings deepened. He knew of his special relationship to his Father and was absorbed with his Father's nearness and his love for him; he experienced the Father as
no one ever had experienced or known him. As St. Paul insists,
"Though he was by nature God, he did not consider being equal
to God a thing to be clung to, but rather he emptied himself, taking on the nature of a servant" (Phil 2:6–7). His closeness to his

Father did not set him apart or distance him from those near him, but rather his closeness to the Father drew him nearer to them. His heart was full of the love of his Father for every creature; he saw beauty in the disfigured, peace in the troubled, love in the tormented. He was drawn most to those who seemed farthest away from him and his Father—the outcasts, the psychotic, the prostitutes—drawing them into the love and acceptance which went out from him, and in so doing drawing them to the Father.

Since Jesus Christ fully shared our human condition, he had to face all the ambiguity, the complexity, the challenge which comes with being human. He had to face rejection, abuse and persecution throughout his life, and finally death itself. As terrified as he was of the death that awaited him, he faced it out of fidelity and love. All that he had taught, all that he had stood for, all that his Father's faithful love promised, would have meant nothing if he had abandoned his mission and abandoned his friends at the moment of testing. "He loved those who were his own, and he loved them to the very end." If he had run and hidden—looked out for number one—he would have been no Lord, no brother. He demonstrated his solidarity with us in our weakness and fear, by accepting death, even death on a cross. His death summed up his whole life. If he had flown off like the clay birds at the moment of testing, his life and death would have been something beyond us.

His Father saw his faithful love until the end, and was truly pleased with him, and accordingly raised him to new life on that first Easter Sunday. The resurrection is the Father's affirmation of Jesus and the way he lived. The promise of Easter for us is that if we remain faithful to the Father like Jesus, even in the face of suffering and death, we too will know resurrection and new life.

There's a story told about St. Teresa of Avila, the great seventeenth century reformer of the Carmelite convents of Spain, who was crossing a narrow bridge on her horse, and the bridge collapsed under her. As she was spitting out water and struggling to stay afloat in the water, she looked up to heaven and said, "God, if this is the way you treat your friends, no wonder you have so few of them." We might look at the life of Jesus and say, "God, if this is how you treat your only Son, no wonder you have so few sons and daughters." Yet our faith tells us that the Father invites each one of us to walk the same path his Son walked, no more, no less. He invites us to come to him by way of suffering and death like his only Son. There is no other way. We say to ourselves, "Yes, I know that. Yes, I know that every human life must have its full share of suffering and pain. Yet, I know that there is no real human depth, no human richness without pain and suffering." Yet when it comes our way, we shout immediately, "Why me, Lord? Why can't I live happily ever after like so-and-so down the street? Why do I have to endure all this rejection, heartbreak and fear?"

In every age, our faith tells us that for some unknown reason God invites some to walk more closely, to know more pain, to be put more clearly to the test. Their suffering is for the others, as Christ's suffering was for us. In some way their rejection, betrayal and abandonment are an invitation for others to come to faith and know the Lord. Could it be in our time that many of our divorced brothers and sisters are invited to mirror the suffering and death of Christ in their own lives—and to come to new life afterward—as a sign that God is present to our suffering and drawing men and women to himself? The suffering of divorce is not then a sign that God does not love me, but that his love for me as a divorced person is so great that he calls me to show forth in my life his healing, renewing love for all.

The suffering of divorced men and women is much like the suffering of Jesus himself. He endured rejection, abandonment, death; we in turn find ourselves rejected by our spouse and dropped by friends, and with a dead marriage. In the depths of that suffering we remember that Jesus truly went through the same thing; we have in him a brother in this suffering. So rather than becoming estranged from God at this time and asking "Why did you let this happen to me, God?" our response might well be: "I have a hard time being grateful to you, Lord, for this suffering I'm going through. I wish it could all pass away, but if it must be, I accept it, and I trust that your love will see me through all this, and help me become a stronger, better person in the process—a better person for myself and a better person for others."

"Did you look like that, Lord? Did you look so abandoned, so rejected, so despised? That's what I look like now. But with you beside me, I know I will make it, and I know that somewhere at the end of this dark tunnel of suffering is the light of resurrection and new life. Help me through the night, Lord."

Trust

A smartly-dressed young executive named Michael came to see me one day; his wife had left him after four years of marriage. "What really hurt, Father, was that she had planned it for a full year, and I never suspected anything. She was already packed the morning she told me, and had already rented a new apartment. 'No hard feelings,' she said as she left. 'I just don't want to be married anymore.' I felt so stupid, so angry, I swore that I'd never trust another woman as long as I lived. What's worse, I stopped trusting God anymore or even trusting myself." He told me that he had spent two tours of duty as a combat Marine in Vietnam, but that this divorce was harder.

Many people insist after a divorce that they'll never trust anyone again; they feel betrayed and used. Their lack of trust seems to be infectious, spreading out into the whole range of their relationships—to friends, relatives, and even God. Rejection by the person one loved can be devastating, and the trauma that follows the breakdown of a marriage and separation, especially when it is unwanted, can make people question everything in life—all their values, all their goals, all their assumptions about life. The Chinese word for crisis is made up of two different characters put together; one character means danger, and the other means opportunity. The crisis of divorce brings with it the danger that one will become cynical, disillusioned, permanently distrustful; it can also bring with it the opportunity to learn the real meaning of trust and to be more successful at trusting in the future.

The most taunting question at first is usually, "Why did I trust this person I married?" What qualities had he or she demonstrated to make them worthy of my trust? A woman psychiatrist friend of mine, who has been divorced twice herself, says that everyone has to admit that we got married for what we were going to get out of it. Maybe we were looking forward to just being married, to sexual fulfillment, to having children, to being able to socialize as a couple, to feeling loved by someone. Falling in love necessarily involves a certain over-idealization of the other person. Michael remembered when he couldn't figure out why everyone else couldn't see his fiancée's marvelous qualities.

Several years ago on a trip to Alaska I met with about 150 high school juniors and seniors, and in our discussion I asked them how they would know when they had found the right person to marry, someone they could really trust. They looked at me blank-faced, and then looked at one another as if to suggest that this priest was really out of it. Several then volunteered, "You just know!" The romantic illusion—that is, the belief that when the right person for me comes along I'll know—remains remarkably strong in our society even though we've lived for a generation with so much divorce.

Michael later told me it took two years of therapy before he could face the fact that he was attracted to exactly the wrong kind of woman for him. He had been involved in a second live-in relationship with another woman before that fact came crashing home. He learned that in a strange way, the women he was attracted to had many qualities similar to his mother, with whom he had never gotten along very well. After a lot of therapy, insight and support he began to build some more successful relationships with different kinds of women.

One of the surprising effects of the breakup of his marriage for Michael was that he also lost trust in his friends. "These were guys and gals I hung out with a lot," he said, "lots of parties and picnics, lots of serious conversations about politics, sports, business—a great gang! But when my life collapsed, except for one or two, I became about as welcome as herpes. I began to see that we were great at hanging around together, but there wasn't any real depth to our relationships. I met one guy I hadn't seen in months at a party, and he looked embarrassed, and then haltingly offered, "Well, I've really been thinking about you, and I heard it's really been heavy for you, but . . . "

Michael told me that he also started spending time alone in empty churches. "Maybe it was that old Catholic smell that was comforting. I even went to confession once when I really had nothing to confess. Even though I didn't consider myself particularly religious, somehow I believed that getting married in church guaranteed that my marriage would last. I prayed my knees off that she would reconsider and come back, and that we could make it again, but she didn't. I began to get really angry with God, but didn't know how to handle it. I finally began sitting in Church and telling him off. He took it pretty well!

"Worst of all," he continued, "I began to realize that I was beginning to distrust myself—I had come a long way banking on a good set of life instincts, and now I was beginning to wonder if I was really in touch at all. Had I really been living in a dreamworld?"

The difference came when a guy in the business reached out to him. "He'd been through a worse divorce than mine. He took me seriously, seemed to understand what was going on. We talked a lot; he let me call at crazy hours, and he listened. He shared what he had been through, but didn't tell me what I should do. He took me to this divorced Catholics group; I really expected to find a crowd of broken wings, but that wasn't the case. They were a pretty down-to-earth group, including some very successful people, and, more than that, some very nice people, and they welcomed me and made me feel at home. I didn't feel so much alone."

One night, after a meeting at the church, Michael went with about eight people to a local watering hole for beer and oysters. "I'll never forget it. I guess I led the conversation, and I put on the table the whole issue of trust: 'How do you begin to trust again?' I'll never forget it. This wonderful gal with a baritone voice who sold computers answered, 'You just do. You put your hands over your head, and go head-first like the first time you ever dove into water. What's the alternative? Going through life being suspicious of everyone and everything and, most of all, yourself?' And somebody else chimed in, 'You have to start trusting again, but maybe this time because of all you've been through, you trust smarter. You throw away the rose-colored glasses, and check people out. You learn to test relationships, and learn to test yourself. Refusing to trust again is to remain alone, isolated, sick.' "

Michael then told me of a surprising religious experience that happened to him one Sunday evening at Mass. The folk group was leading a song and the words touched him deeply:

He will raise you on eagle's wings,
  Bear you on the breath of dawn,
Make you to shine like the sun,
  And hold you in the palm of his hand.

"Here I was looking for a reason to trust God again, and it suddenly struck me how much God loved and trusted me. He'd given me lots of space to work out my life; he hadn't laid it all out for me; he had even let me mess it up in some ways. Despite all that, he still loves me and cares for me and believes in me. I began to see that trust in God didn't mean that everything worked our perfectly for us, but that God was with us however it went, and was always ready to help us grow through the worst that could happen to us."

Michael and I talked several times over the year or more that he was getting his life together. He told me that he began to see that trust in God, trust in others, and trust in self were all pieces of the same pie. He began to see that as he found new friends who cared for him and helped him trust in people again, he began to be able to deal with the issue of trusting in God, and then, with lots of help from therapist, friends and God, he began to trust in himself again. "I see now," he said, "that you can't work out the trust issue on any one level alone. It requires work on all these fronts. It doesn't come easily, and there may even be some setbacks with some new bad experiences, but by concentrating on God and friends and myself, it gradually began to come together.

"One day over lunch, a college friend whom I hadn't seen in several years told me that I'd really changed. He said he couldn't quite put his finger on it, but I seemed different, more together, more at peace. I laughed and said that if he really knew what a mess I was, he'd never say that, but down deep I knew he was right, that it was beginning to come together."

There are no reasons that *make* trust inevitable. There are only reasons and people who invite trust. Trust is always an invitation to place ourselves in another's hands. When it is a well-placed trust, the peace and contentment it brings produce the deepest sense of well-being. "Yet," as Michael says now, "you learn that you never bat a thousand at trust. The give and take of life, growing and becoming an adult, all involve tension, failure, mistakes. You learn to be more savvy as time goes on, but at some point it's like that trust exercise they have on those sensitivity training weekends—you check out the people around you, and make sure they have strong arms, but then you just have to lie backward and let yourself fall into their arms. There just doesn't seem to be any other way."

Forgiveness

*I*n the spring of 1983 I preached at the annual Bishop's Mass for the Divorced in the diocese of Wilmington, Delaware. The Gospel reading that day was on forgiveness, a text chosen by the planning committee of the local divorce group. I began my homily by recalling a woman who once said to me, "Father, I'll never be able to forgive my husband, because I'll never be able to forget what he did to me." I suggested that forgiveness is not amnesia—it doesn't mean blotting out the past. Rather forgiveness means beginning to look at the past in a new way. For the person who has forgiven, the past becomes constructive, not destructive.

Divorced people, I continued, know so well the danger of dwelling on the past, of becoming absorbed in each and every hurt, of continually going over and over every wrong. Some people never stop scoring points, proving their former spouse wrong. Their view of the past is full of "if only's." Such obsession can lead to simmering anger, bitterness, even hatred. It can have dangerous physical and psychological effects on the one who can't forgive. In this case the past can never become a source of self-knowledge and growth.

"Forgiveness is an act of love—love of God, love of self, love of one's former spouse. It is an act of love toward one who has injured us. Such love goes beyond our human instincts and abilities. Such love bears out the old saying, 'To err is human, to forgive is divine.' "

I concluded by pointing out that the reason we need to forgive those who have injured us is because we have been forgiven ourselves. Jesus in his ministry was the embodiment of forgiveness, God's forgiveness in the flesh. Again and again in his ministry we find him announcing to suffering people, "Your sins are forgiven." He insists again and again, "You are loved; you are accepted; you are the children of my heavenly Father who loves you without condition." He came among us as the divine physician to heal our injuries and bring us pardon and peace. "As you have been forgiven, so must you forgive one another." He helped us see that by forgiving one another, we are most like a forgiving God.

After that Mass was over, a woman came up to me to say: "Father, I knew just what you were talking about. My husband, Joseph, left me after 22 years of marriage for another woman. He still hasn't married her. I hated him; I was tied up in knots of bitterness and anger. I don't think I realized how sour I had become. One morning I went to Mass on my way to work as I often do. It was the feast of Saint Joseph, and so I stopped at St. Joseph's altar after Mass and lit a candle. I was praying for peace and health, and all of a sudden I heard a voice. 'Forgive Joseph.' That's right. I heard the voice as clear as if it was you talking. 'Forgive Joseph.' So I did, and everything changed for the better. I felt as though I had turned it all around. I felt free. The burden of the past seemed to be lifted off my shoulders. Over the coming months I began to find new energy for myself and my kids. He hasn't been any easier to relate to, but I feel differently toward him, more patient, more understanding. He still bugs me at times, but he can't upset me the way he could before I'd forgiven him."

My Wilmington friend expressed better what I was trying to say in that homily at Mass. I've repeated that Wilmington story several times since in talks I've given on forgiveness. I always try to center my remarks around the meaning of forgiveness in the life of Jesus. Jesus had to forgive too. Remember when he was in his final agony, when he was beaten and publicly humiliated, and all his friends ran for the hills. They obviously were weak and afraid. Even on Easter Sunday when the women told them that they had seen the Lord and he was alive, they were still afraid, and stayed huddled behind locked doors in the upper room. Then Jesus came and stood in their midst. He didn't say to them, "I forgive you for abandoning me, you weaklings." He could have rubbed it in, but he didn't. He said: "Receive the Holy Spirit; whose sins you forgive, they are forgiven." His message was: "You know you're forgiven—wasn't that what my ministry was all about? Now that you've experienced the meaning of forgiveness, go and announce my forgiveness to others. Share with others the love and acceptance you have received from me." From day one the early Church was a forgiven people announcing God's forgiveness and love to a world hungering for mercy. The Apostles could never look down their noses at anybody else—or claim that anybody else didn't deserve forgiveness—for they had abandoned the Lord, and they were not only forgiven, but sent to announce the Lord's forgiveness of all. Jesus even put the best interpretation on their abandonment when he said from the cross, "Father, forgive them, for they do not know what they are doing."

There is another scene which brings out the quality of the Lord's forgiveness beautifully—the story of the two disciples whom Jesus meets on the first Easter Sunday on the road to Emmaus. Two disciples, obviously heartbroken and desolate, are walking from Jerusalem to Emmaus. Their life has collapsed. All they had dreamed and hoped for has been put to death on Calvary two days before. As they're walking along, a stranger unobtrusively joins them. He asks why they look so downhearted, and they look at him wide-eyed, asking if he's the only person in these parts that doesn't know what happened these past few days. "What things?" the stranger asks. And they go on to tell him about Jesus of Nazareth, a man mighty in word and deed, and how they had hoped he was the one who would set Israel free, but now he has been crucified and all seems lost.

The stranger then begins to relate the Scriptures to them about how the Messiah had to be a suffering servant, not a mighty ruler, and how he would lay down his life for his people to help them see that they must lay down their lives in love for one another. The disciples are entranced by the insights of the stranger, and slowly the confused events of the past few days begin to make sense. After a while the stranger makes signs of moving on, and they beg him to share some supper with them at the inn of Emmaus; they obviously want to talk more. When they get to table, the stranger takes bread, blesses it, breaks it, and gives it to them. Immediately their eyes are opened, and they recognize the Lord in the breaking of the bread.

How does the Lord respond to those who have injured him and abandoned him? He ministers to them, he serves them, he teaches them. He walks with them as one who has forgiven them, as one who loves them even more in their frailty. He doesn't forget everything that happened these past few days, but rather he explains to them the meaning of his death and resurrection for them. His death was not the end for him; it need not be the end for them. If they will accept his forgiveness, and go forth as men and women who have been forgiven, they can change their own lives and change the world.

Forgiving former spouses who have injured us or hurt us doesn't mean blotting out what they have done or even adopting a permissive attitude toward them. Our forgiveness doesn't make them different persons. The most painful aspect of such forgiveness may be that it may not be reciprocated—there may be no sign that a former spouse has forgiven us or looks at us differently. We don't forgive to win forgiveness in return, but rather to move closer to God who is all-forgiving. There is also a kind of helplessness about forgiveness, for we can often do very little for former spouses. Their growth must be their own; we can't embark on some crusade to straighten them out. We must respect the distance the divorce has brought, and pray that it be not a hostile distance but, at least from our side, a distance of peace.

The story of my Wilmington friend who forgave Joseph seems to indicate that forgiveness takes only a moment. It's true that there is a key moment of decision that helps us cross the threshold from bitterness to forgiveness. But there is much that prepares for that moment, and much that helps us be faithful to that moment after it's made. My Wilmington friend said she often prayed and often went to daily Mass; she said she wasn't praying specifically for the grace of forgiveness, but yet I think that when we open our hearts to God in prayer, we automatically pray for the things we truly need. The ability to forgive was the answer to prayer for this woman even though she may never have articulated it as such. There had been much preparation for that moment of key insight which changed her life. After she had made it, I'm sure there were many temptations to turn back and pick up the old, familiar behaviors of bitterness. She may even have slipped occasionally into that old behavior, it runs so deep.

Forgiveness is a gift from God. " . . . to forgive is divine." We need to pray for that gift, confident that God will give us the things we truly need. Such prayer may well prepare our hearts for a very difficult wrenching of gears and change of attitude. Such prayer might well focus on Jesus forgiving from the cross, or announcing forgiveness to his friends in the upper room on Easter, or helping the disciples on the road to Emmaus. What we do in forgiving one another is imitate Christ. My Wilmington friend's great breakthrough came after attending Mass. How wonderfully appropriate! At Mass when we recall the supper Jesus shared with his disciples on the night before he died, we repeat again those powerful words he spoke over the cup of wine:

"This is my blood which is shed for the forgiveness of sins." He is saying: "My blood, my whole life was lived and poured out so that you might know forgiveness and be able to forgive one another."

Sometimes this process of forgiveness can be helped if we find someone to share our struggle with. The person we talk with might be another divorced friend or a Church minister, a lay counselor, a priest or a sister. Sometimes we very much need the encouragement and support of another at this difficult time just as the disciples on the road needed the stranger to explain to them all that had happened.

Forgiveness doesn't come easily, nor, once it is done, does it make everything easy, but it is the only way to know the peace the Lord offered to his huddled, fearful disciples on that first Easter when he stood in their midst and said, "Peace be with you."

Temptation

"*D*oes recovery after divorce always bring with it a more loving, fulfilling life?" Arthur asked me. "Not necessarily," I responded, as I have so often when a similar question is asked. I went on to explain that the process of recovery can be subtly sabotaged into a new self-centeredness, an enlightened "looking out for Number One." Some people adjust, put on a new face, resolve never to get hurt again, learn to cope with style, but really don't recover. Their adjustment has all the appearances of recovery, but their hearts are hollow. I'm reminded of the haunting words from T.S. Eliot's *Murder in the Cathedral*, "The last temptation is the greatest treason, to do the right thing for the wrong reason." What are the right reasons, the right motives that should shape real recovery? I shared with Art some thought on the temptations of Jesus which provide some insight.

After Jesus had been baptized by his cousin John at the beginning of his ministry, the Spirit led Jesus into the desert to be tempted: "The Spirit immediately drove him out into the wilderness. And he was in the wilderness forty days, tempted by Satan" (Mt 4). It is a dramatic scene: Jesus, ever the devout Jew, reliving the experience of Moses and the Jewish people in the desert, spending hours on end in prayerful communion with his Father, preparing for his coming ministry. He fasts to purify his senses and relieve sluggishness; what his Father is asking of him begins to come into clearer focus. He begins to see that his Father is not asking him to be a mighty warrior king who will restore Israel to earthly prominence and drive away the hated Romans; what he is asking is linked to those favorite poems from Isaiah the prophet which run through his thoughts. He cannot hide from the disconcerting image of Isaiah's suffering servant—the man of sorrows, rejected and abused, who suffers silently for his people. Jesus begins to see in the desert that he is called to invite the people of Israel to "trod the winepress" with him, to walk the humble, sorrowful way of faith that alone leads to salvation. As the Spirit gives him insight, he all too humanly begins to shrink in fear, flooded with inadequacy. He is tempted—tempted to compromise, water down his mandate, become an all-too-earthly, crowd-pleasing Messiah.

The three temptations which Jesus confronts in the desert at the beginning of his ministry are three temptations that come to anyone struggling to live as a Christian, three temptations that come most seductively to the recovering divorced persons. Jesus is tempted to selfishness, control and reputation, all aspects of doing the right thing for the wrong reason.

First, Jesus is tempted by Satan to selfishness. "If you are the Son of God, command these stones to become loaves of bread." But Jesus answers him, "Man shall not live by bread alone but by every word that proceeds from the mouth of God." Jesus is tempted to use his power to feed himself, not God's hungry people. Art remembered thinking to himself: "I'm not going to be a chump any longer; from now on I'm putting Number One first." It's an inevitable temptation after the searing pain of divorce. After having felt betrayed, rejected, abused, one easily finds a little selfishness in order. Art thought, "I'm just not going to let myself get hurt again; I'm just not getting involved. That's all fine for other people, but not for me anymore. Nice guys finish last." The temptation may not be that explicit; it may be more a subtle undercurrent of withdrawal and narrow self-interest. It may be the continuing avoidance of the tasks of reconnection and reconciliation with family and friends; it may be an intense self-absorption with my exercise, and my recreation, and my education, and my job, and my playtime, and "I'm sorry but other people are simply going to have take a back seat for a time." What's subtle about this temptation is that there is some truth in all of the above; for men and women who have never taken themselves seriously and never taken good care of themselves, there is a need for serious attention to self at this troubled time. It's the right thing to do, but it can be done for the wrong reason. The wrong reason is doing everything for oneself alone; the right reason is to set aside the necessary time for personal recovery—counseling, school, recreation—but all aimed at getting back into circulation, learning to love more effectively, building a new social network, learning to be giving again.

Second, Jesus is tempted to control and worldly power. The devil took him to the holy city, and set him on the pinnacle of the temple, and said to him, "If you are the Son of God, throw yourself down; for it is written: 'He will give his angels charge of you,' and 'On their hands they will bear you up lest you strike your foot against a stone.' " Jesus is tempted to use the power given him by his Father for himself rather than for others. He is tempted to control, to set it up his own way, to protect himself, rather than identify with the weak and the powerless. It's such a subtle temptation. What refuge would the fallen and suffering find in a mighty ruler; their search is always for one who will be with them in their suffering.

For the recovering divorced person, this second temptation leads one to assert control and be in charge, rather than ever again appear vulnerable and possibly be hurt. Art recognized how he had tried to be the person who has it all together, knows all the rules of the road, and has learned all the lessons of being divorced. Art saw that he was becoming the kind of person who's hard to come close to, to make friends with, to cry on his shoulder. Again this is doing the right thing for the wrong reason. Getting one's act together and learning to stand on one's own two feet is an essential part of the recovery process, but doing it in such a way as to appear to wear a new suit of armor is ultimately self-defeating. There is a subtle difference here between the recovering person who has it too much together, and the recovering person who is doing very well, but is ready to be open to those who are still hurting. Real healing and togetherness, the kind that runs deep in the personality, makes us gentle and caring for others in need, just as Jesus in his ministry did not "lord it over" the people he was sent to serve, but became one with them in their illness, their brokenness, their homelessness. So true recovery doesn't set us above or beyond others who are hurting, but rather joins us to them in Christian love.

Third, Jesus is tempted to care about his reputation, what others think of him. "Again the devil took him to a very high mountain, and showed him all the kingdoms of the world and the glory of them; and he said to him: 'All these I will give you, if you will fall down and worship me.' Then Jesus said to him, 'Begone, Satan! for it is written, You shall worship the Lord your God and him only shall you serve.' " Jesus is tempted to pervert his calling into a kind of glory parade—to elicit applause, play to the bleachers, develop a devoted, adoring following, be busy, be needed, be the "good rabbi," rather than say the hard things and confront the powers of darkness and risk disapproval, identify with the friendless.

We find Jesus throughout the Gospels in battle with the forces of evil which would pervert and destroy his ministry. Here in the third temptation comes possibly the most perverse, the most subtle challenge. Do it all so that others will think well of you. Art began to see that the trap is to fall back into a life which had entrapped him once before—trying to live a script written by others, rather than owning one's own uniqueness and special personal identity. He saw that the temptation is to become the perfect divorced person, the healed and integrated and new-again Arthur—living off what others think rather than rooting one's life in what one knows about one's self, and ultimately what one knows about God.

We talked about how appropriate it is to care about what others think, to be concerned about one's reputation, to accept the sincere praise that can come from becoming a new person. But doing the right thing for the wrong reason means being seduced by the approval of others and failing to concentrate on doing the right thing for the right reason: striving for that human wholeness which is worthwhile in itself whatever others think. It is this personal integrity which enables us to risk the disapproval of others and not be turned upside down by every trendy definition of wholeness which comes along. It is this attitude which enables us to develop a spiritual core, such as Jesus had.

Doing right or wrong is often not a simple either/or thing. It may well be that some aspects of our behavior, which later we believe are wrong, were the best possible at the moment, and actually led in time to our acting more authentically. Art recalled how in the early months after his separation, when he was still seething with anger, he went frantically to every party and every outing, almost shouting out, "Hey, look at me! I'm alive! I'm making it!" He was not really doing all that well, but it was a necessary response to rejection. Yet he saw later that he needed all that activity to survive. "I found that my behavior and my reasons got 'righter' as I got more healed," he told me. "I had to learn to love myself all over again, for my sense of myself was like an eggshell, so fragile and ready to crack. I used to quote the old Braniff ad, 'If you've got it, flaunt it!' That 'flaunting it' helped me strengthen my fragility and begin to get it together."

Some people feel so guilty about doing anything for themselves, that they seem to freeze in the recovery process. Any time they spend a dollar on themselves or take some time off, the old guilt kicks into gear. My friend, psychologist Pat Livingston, insists that divorcing people have such a great need to care for themselves at this time. It's good to have a vision of what the right reasons for shaping recovery are, but we must be patient with ourselves as we struggle to get by on some fairly flawed motives. The right reasons fall into place in time.

Art said this is so hard—doing the right thing for the right reason. The world is so full of temptation to undermine the work of the Spirit in our lives. For the Spirit calls us to become authentically ourselves, authentically the person only we can become. To sustain such a genuine process of true Christian recovery requires first of all the same discipline we see in Jesus in the desert: quiet, regular, prayerful communion with the Father, and discipline in eating, sleeping, and drinking—habits which can, when uncontrolled, lead to sluggishness, dullness of vision, blindness to temptation.

Secondly, this genuine Christian recovery can only be sustained in the context of community. We need our quiet, thoughtful times alone and apart, but we, like Jesus, need companions in the process, trusted men and women committed like ourselves to a Christian life, people we can pray with and share with and find support with. Searching out soulmates, whom we can share our slippage with and share a step ahead with, is also crucial to the process; such soulmates may be trusted friends, a spiritual director, a priest. Jesus showed us in the desert that we must not hide from the terrors, the temptations that come to us when alone. At those dark moments we must trust the love of the Father who is always present to hold us up and help us carry through.

Art is a quiet man, who never blows his own horn, but after people get to know him, they often remark that he is well put together. He usually does the right thing for the right reason.

Prayer

"At times when the stress seemed almost unbearable, I got an old rosary out of the drawer and said it over and over again. The repetitiousness of it and the familiar prayers were comforting." Many people like Fred who rediscovered the rosary have told me that at similar difficult moments after separation they drew upon the prayers of their childhood, or began to go to Mass more often, or joined a prayer group—and all these things helped. I remember Jane who told me that she felt so funny about her relationship with God after her husband left—so ambivalent, so angry—that she just couldn't deal with God, and decided not to go to Mass or even speak to him for a year. "I knew that when the year was up, he'd still be there, and maybe then I could deal with him."

Prayer in all shapes and forms becomes an important resource for many divorcing people, and difficulty with prayer comes to many. Some find themselves on their knees praying that God will turn it all around and heal the separation. Others plead for strength and courage and an end to bitterness and recrimination. Still others say that they find no suitable words for what they're feeling, and they just sit silently, hoping God is with them. Some say that they hadn't prayed in years, and just didn't know how to do it anymore; the childhood ways didn't seem adequate, and if there were some new ways, they didn't know them. Others say restlessness, emotional ups and downs, and the regularity of the irregular sabotage many resolutions to pray more often.

Many of us know lots of prayers by memory, but really don't know how to pray very well. I can remember being taught in second grade that prayer is "lifting up our minds and hearts to God." That captures it very well. Prayer is a way of getting in contact with God. It may mean getting away alone in some quiet space, and sitting in the warmth of God's loving presence, the way one sits comfortably in the living room of a close friend. One may spend quiet time with God or one may naturally try to express feelings in words or familiar prayers. But prayer can also be, and may more often be, those moments in the midst of the swim of our daily lives when God breaks in and we experience his presence. It may be listening to a friend share some ordinary little event of life or watching a child climb a tree or sitting at a traffic light and remembering a stranger's kindness. "The whole world is charged with the presence of God," the poet Gerard Manley Hopkins observed. Prayer is all those times we tune in and are touched by God's abiding love.

Prayer requires practice, like running or knitting or playing the clarinet. Amid all the busyness and distractions of our daily lives, especially the hectic pace that comes after divorce, it is essential to carve out some special moments and some private space that's reserved for oneself and God. It may mean taking advantage of little private moments while shaving or dressing or ironing; it may mean taking advantage of a walk down a flight of stairs or a ride to work. Prayer may be hard to remember with all the other things on one's mind, but the rewards for the divorcing in perspective and peace can be very great.

"I really don't know how to speak with God," Fred told me. "I'm not good at remembering prayers, and I don't seem to be able to express the things on my mind the way I would like."

"Why don't you say that to God?" I replied. "God's not marking our grammar, and he knows that many of the intense feelings we're experiencing are hard to express. We may not have a very good handle on them ourselves. Why don't you tell him that?"

"Prayer is not time that I give to God, but rather time that God gives to me. I find it's up to me to accept it as a gift." With that thought Mary had begun to understand that prayer was not something she owed God, or something that good Christians were supposed to do. Rather prayer is a time God gives to her; it's like a private audience with a very important person—a time when I open myself to God's loving presence. "Prayer," Mary observed, "is opening our hearts to God so that he can come in and bring us the peace which is his gift."

The prayer of the Church is first and foremost the celebration of the Eucharist. At Mass it is Christ who prays to his Father on our behalf and invites us to unite ourselves with him in his prayer. His word gives shape and meaning to our feeble words. Learning to be more attentive and present to the prayer of Christ in the Eucharist can be an important way of growing in prayerfulness. Maybe getting to church a few minutes early before Mass begins and taking time to quiet down can be an excellent preparation. Concentrating on the Scripture readings and being attentive to the spoken responses; uniting oneself with the movements of the Mass—the offering of gifts, the elevation of the bread and cup, the breaking of the bread; uniting oneself with the movements of one's heart—offering oneself to God, raising up one's thoughts to God, and sharing one's life with others—all these can deepen one's prayerfulness. At the beginning of the Communion rite we repeat the prayer that Jesus gave us. He said, "Now while you pray, don't prattle as do the pagans who believe they will be heard because of their many words. Don't imitate them, for your Father knows what you need even before you ask him. Pray like this:

    'Our Father who art in heaven,
        hallowed be thy name.

Thy kingdom come.
Thy will be done on earth as it is in heaven.
Give us this day our daily bread,
and forgive us our trespasses,
as we forgive those who trespass against us.
And lead us not into temptation,
    but deliver us from the evil one.' "

The Lord's Prayer invites us, first of all, to let God be God. "Lord, I worship you. You are to be praised for all your love and mercy. May your kingdom, your will for all humankind, come on earth and in heaven. Despite the mess which my life seems to be in, I find clarity and peace in you, and praise you. I know I depend on you for everything, and you depend on me to accept the life you have given me as it is and make something of it: 'Give us this day our daily bread.' Make me a forgiving person, for I know I am unable to pray—to really live—unless I have a forgiving heart. Help me to forgive those who have injured me, and help those whom I have injured to forgive me, so that we can live in peace. Protect me, Lord, from all the temptations that are around me and save me from evil."

I can remember hearing a particularly painful confession one day, and, after a long dialogue, suggesting to the penitent that he say one "Our Father" as his penance. "Is that all I have to do?" he asked. "Say it slowly, thoughtfully. Let the sentiments sink in," I responded. "Say it several times if you like, but if you could get the meaning of that prayer into your heart, you would be a changed man."

Many divorced Catholics have found great spiritual nourishment in belonging to prayer groups, yet I have found others who are not comfortable with such groups. I like to point out the danger of spiritual elitism—i.e., thinking that some ways of praying are superior to others. Some people thrive on intense spiritual involvement and become very active in prayer groups. I thank God that they have found such powerful spiritual support. But many others seem to go their own way spiritually, carving out their own prayer rhythms and finding their own comfortable prayer forms. Just as God made no two of us alike, so no two ways of communicating with God are meant to be alike. The key, I think, is for everyone to connect with God in his or her own way. Some spend much more time at it than others; some raise their arms while praying when others prefer to go unnoticed; some find silence the best way of coming close while others find they pray best while doing some act of charity for others. Prayer is not a method; it is each person's unique relationship with God.

Last year Mother Teresa of Calcutta came to Washington and was received by Senator Mark Hatfield of Oregon on Capitol Hill. "I've been to India, Mother Teresa, and seen the enormous problems of poverty and disease that you and your sisters face. You must find so little success confronting such enormous ills. How do you keep going?"

"Senator," she answered, "God does not expect us to be successful, only faithful."

God doesn't expect our prayer to be successful, whatever that might mean, but only faithful. Sticking to it as we change and grow and accordingly as the style and shape of our prayer shifts and develops is the key. The kind of prayer that worked in the stressful months after separation may not work three years later, but the key is to keep praying in ever new ways so that God's presence to our growing and becoming is always before our minds and hearts.

Like so many divorced people I have known, Fred became a very prayerful man. "It's not something I have to do," he told me, "but it's become part of the way I live." Fred says that when

he finds divorced friends struggling to learn to pray, he suggests
the Prayer of Saint Francis:

> Lord, make me an instrument of your peace.
> Where there is hatred, let me sow love.
> Where there is injury, pardon;
> Where there is doubt, faith;
> Where there is despair, hope;
> Where there is darkness, light;
> And where there is sadness, joy.
>
> O Divine Master, grant that I may not so much
> Seek to be consoled as to console;
> To be understood as to understand;
> To be loved as to love;
> For it is in giving that we receive,
> It is in pardoning that we are pardoned,
> And in dying that we are born to eternal life.

Celibacy

"*I* was told by a priest, now that I'm separated from my wife, that I'm supposed to live a celibate life," Doug told me on a retreat weekend. "I'm sorry, but I think I know myself, and there's no way I can be celibate. I guess I'll just have to leave the Church."

Are separated and divorced persons supposed to live celibate lives? I think I surprised Doug by telling him that the breakdown of a marriage does not bring with it the gift of celibacy. I went on to explain that the Church has always taught that celibacy is a gift given to a few by God for the building up of his presence on earth. The Church has never held that it is a gift widely given, and it has never taught that it comes automatically with a broken marriage.

For the past six years I've been involved in training young men for the priesthood in the Paulist Order, and I have been charged by my superiors and by the Church to ascertain whether the young men who join our order have the necessary strengths to live a celibate life. For the last thousand years the Roman Catholic Church has linked priestly ministry with the gift of celibacy. What do we look for to determine if a young man has what it takes to receive the gift of celibacy? You might think offhand that we look for a young man who has never dated or has never had sexual thoughts or is fairly reserved in his social behavior. Nothing could be farther from the truth. A young man like that would probably not function very well as a priest; he'd have a hard time responding warmly and humanly to the many people who come to him for help. What we look for is a young man with real warmth of personality, with good social skills, one who may have dated and thought seriously of marrying, but one who is willing to sacrifice wife and family and give himself completely to the service of God's people. It's not always immediately evident whether a young man has such a gift. That's why the Church takes four years or more to help him test his calling and discover whether he has the requisite resources to be a genuine, caring, celibate minister for God's people. We know that what God and the Church is asking of this young man is very hard. He is asked to be part of many families yet a member of none; he is asked to offer emotional nurture to all who come to him weary and hurting; he is asked to develop a difficult, unique support system of friends to sustain him, all the while putting his ultimate trust in the Lord who has called him to this demanding way of life.

When you examine how careful the Church is about letting young men who desire to be priests take the vow of celibacy, it's easy to see why I insist that broken marriage doesn't automatically bring with it the gift of celibacy. To say so would diminish the value of celibacy and lay an unfair burden on the divorced. This does not mean that I have not met separated and divorced men and women who are leading lives marked by genital sexual abstinence, and have freely chosen to do so, convinced that it is contributing to their personal well-being.

Psychologists who work with divorcing persons report that the time after divorce is often filled with sexual tension. For some men and women who experienced a decrease in sexual interest and activity when their marriage was coming apart, they find the time after separation marked by an increase in sexual interest. They find themselves becoming erotically alive again. It may well be that their new freedom from stress and a relationship that contributed to a bad self-image may enable them to look more positively at themselves sexually.

A psychologist, Dr. Martha Cleveland, says that the sexual behavior of divorcing persons she has counseled reveals several basic motivational factors. First of all, there is a strong need for companionship, intimacy, and emotional affirmation. They feel overwhelmed with loneliness and very rejected. Secondly, there is a strong need in many people to become involved sexually as a way of blotting out the emotional sense of failure which follows the breakup of a marriage. Feeling some sexual pleasure convinces them for a brief time at least that they are not a loser. For some men and women, especially those who experienced sexual abuse or sexual put-downs during the breakup of a marriage, there is a strong need, she insists, for them to affirm their masculinity and femininity, attempting to prove that they could be attractive to another person. Obviously, divorced people once got married because they were convinced that they needed an on-going committed relationship to meet their personal and sexual needs. A failed marriage doesn't erase those emotional needs. Instead, Dr. Cleveland's observation of divorcing people indicates an upsurge in sexual desires and emotional needs following separation, creating a time of great interpersonal vulnerability.

Doug told me he thought he was becoming a sexual pervert, ashamed that he was having so many sexual tensions and problems at this time in his life. I assured him that sexual difficulties at this time are quite normal; such problems only show that he's just like every other divorcing person. He admitted that he had become involved in isolated, short-term sexual encounters or "one-night-stands" looking for sexual release and pleasure, only to find that such relationships only increased his sense of loneliness. The more different sexual partners he had, the more sex became empty and meaningless. When it seemed good on some occasions he was tempted to make too much of the brief encounter, and think of marriage with this person as a way of solving his loneliness. He felt that if he got married it wouldn't be so bad. I shared with him that many observers feel that the high failure rate in second marriages (the failure rate in second marriages in the U.S. is currently higher than the failure rate in first marriages) is related to this "hasty remarriage syndrome" by which many people like Doug rush into a new marriage as a way of meeting their emotional and sexual needs. No one should marry for sex alone, but sometimes unfortunately the divorced are tempted to.

"I think, Doug, there is another way. For many men and women who come through a broken marriage emotionally bruised and shaken, obviously there is no new magical person who's going to make it all better. I remember a young woman who told me that when she finally got up the courage to tell her mother that she was getting a divorce, she said, 'Mom, I think this is the first hurt I've ever had which you can't kiss and make better.' Building a new life after divorce is a long, slow process; it involves restoring your emotional resources and expanding your capacity to relate deeply and meaningfully to other people. A broken marriage may reveal that you were not very good at getting close to other people. How often I've heard people say, 'We were lovers, but never friends.' It is friendship, intimacy, closeness to another that all men and women are looking for, and a broken marriage may reveal intimacy needs you don't know how to meet."

How can one remedy such emotional underdevelopment which becomes apparent after the breakdown of a marriage? Getting emotionally and sexually involved with another person right away is an obvious temptation. It is easy to believe that there is someone out there who's going to make one feel loved and whole again. The truth is most likely that one will only feel loved and whole again if one begins to expand one's own capacity to come close to others and to share deeply with others.

I shared with Doug the story of a divorced friend who invited me to lunch with her on Christmas Eve. When we sat down at a little restaurant, she told me that this was the first Christmas Eve in over twenty years that she had not spent with her husband and children. They had separated two years before, and recently worked out an agreement whereby he would see the children on Christmas Eve this year, and she would see them on Christmas Day. The following year it would be the reverse. As Christmas Eve began to approach she was overwhelmed with anxiety; she told me that I was the only person she could think of who might be free for lunch on Christmas Eve. I was delighted that she thought of me.

As the lunch moved toward dessert she spoke freely about the emotional merry-go-round she had been on since her marriage ended. Her husband was the only person she had ever been sexually intimate with when she separated from him. In the year after, she admitted that she had been involved with about six different men. She felt that she was full of anger and rebellion during that period, but it got "old" very fast. Upon the advice of a friend, she became involved in therapy with a woman psychologist and this relationship became enormously helpful to her. "I've gotten off the mating/dating circuit," she told me. "I realized that I was hiding from myself in these new romantic involvements, and running from the fact that I was hurting. I kept telling myself that there was some man out there who was going to make me feel loved and make me feel beautiful and help me get over all this loneliness and pain. I finally began to see that I was the only one who could help me. I had to find some more successful ways of dealing with my own adjustment problems. I had to grow up and take responsibility for my own emotional well-being." She then admitted that she had not been sexually intimate with a man in nine months.

She went on to describe how building friendships had become her major project. "You know, when we see all male/fe-

male relationships in terms of dating and marriage, we write a
lot of people out of our lives that we wouldn't consider marrying.
I've begun to take interest in many men and women, older and
younger, black and white, of different religions and backgrounds. It's been amazing. I'm finding new friends, real
friends, whom I'd never think of marrying and who aren't interested in marrying me. Some are married, some are divorced,
some single, some widowed, some never married. I've even become buddies with a young male homosexual with whom I work.
We're all interested in each other as persons, not as sexual partners."

She told me that her Divorced Catholics Support Group
had made a great difference for her during this tough time, because these people cared about her as a person and were real
friends. "I'm learning that a good friend is a gift, and having
many friends requires a lot of care and attention. Right now I
think I have more friends than I ever had when I was married.
I'm not suggesting that I'll never remarry, but that's the farthest
thing from my mind right now. I'm enjoying my new-found independence, and I'm discovering parts of myself I never knew
were there. I go to concerts and museums, and read history, and
volunteer at a night school for working mothers. My kids tell me
I've really changed, and they're enjoying me as never before. I
still have sexual tensions like anyone else, but I feel much more
in control."

Doug and I talked about giving up sexual relations as a separated and divorced person, and agreed that it is very hard to
achieve unless one has filled one's life with new sources of intimacy—intimacy with God and intimacy with friends. In pursuit
of personal growth after separation, many men and women I
know are choosing to put aside genital sexual relations not because they're evil or dirty, but because the risk is too great for
them; they don't want to fall into a new dependent relationship
which could stunt their recovery.

Doug readily agreed that this would not be easy. Our sexual needs always reveal our vulnerability and our fragility. Despite our best intentions and our best plans for personal recovery, we often fall. I suggested to him that he find a good confessor or spiritual guide. "We all need someone we can trust, someone we can pour our hearts out to, someone we can tell of our growth and our failures. A good confessor can bring the healing strength of the Lord to us at this tension-filled time, and help us pick up when we fail and help us keep trying," I added.

Such sexual abstinence will not be permanent for many who will remarry, but it will be an important way-station. I like to think that taking one's own sexuality seriously is an essential part of the process of recovery after divorce. Doug wrote to me some months later. He was doing better, and was still in the Church. "I know God's not giving me the gift of celibacy," he wrote. "This growing as a sexual person is very hard. I'm not batting a thousand yet, but I am feeling more together. I'm sure I won't get married for sex alone. I hope to marry again someday, but I know that will be a long time off. What's helping me keep going now is the conviction that God lives and accepts me with all my growing pains and all my slip-ups. I know now he's on my side."

Compassion

We speak often of divorce ministry as a ministry of compassion, since at its heart is that sympathetic, understanding, loving embrace of another in pain. The word itself comes from the Latin which means the capacity "to suffer with" another. It implies that capacity to feel for another, to be moved by another's pain, to see something of oneself in the other, to be touched deeply by the bonds of humanity which link us to one another, and to make each other's pain our own.

Genuine compassion suffers with the other and identifies with the other's hurt, but knows that one cannot take away the other's pain or bear it for that person. There is a false compassion which seeks to erase or blot out or take away another's pain, forgetting that there is nothing that is more one's own than one's pain, and that each of us must confront it and work it through ourselves. Yet the process of recovery is made easier by compassionate friends who encourage and understand what one is going through, and their devotion and fidelity keeps one from falling back and letting the pain take over. The true friend knows that he or she can assist, but that the pain must be worked through at its deepest level alone.

Compassion is a gift, much as artistic sensitivity and human feeling are gifts. Some people seem hardened by the rush of life and come through unreceptive to others' pain; others seem to run away when faced with suffering, while still others pretend to be caring but are never present at the time of need. Still others seem to have radar, are able to see beneath appearances and know when the hurt is intense, and are drawn near the suffering person much as a parent is drawn to a hurting child. They are able to be *with*, to stand beside, linger a while, sit, pray. They usually see themselves not as messiahs or miracle workers, but rather as friends who know intuitively when they are needed, and in what way they are needed. Some people have it, others don't; and sometimes it is hard to figure out why.

It's been said that compassion is caught, not taught, and that some people have personal gifts and temperament strengths which enable them to be more compassionate. It helps to be a feeler and somewhat intuitive in order to be naturally and expressively compassionate. I can remember as a boy hearing my father and mother talk about the poverty, political oppression and numbing work that marked their childhood in Ireland early in this century before the Irish revolution. I caught from them a feeling for working people, poor people, people who were left out. Often people ask me if my parents were divorced. My parents had 43 years of a very happy marriage before my father died in 1974. What I did acquire growing up in their home was a feel for the underdog, for people who had no power or connections or resources to help them in time of need. In my childhood home I vividly remember two prominent pictures, the Sacred Heart and President Franklin D. Roosevelt. Irish Catholicism held then that a loving God in his mercy was on the side of the little guy, the oppressed; and a good society, like the New Deal society, was one where workers and the poor received dignity and rights. This meant to me that God wanted Church people to work for compassionate social change.

Accordingly, I recall from seminary days and all through my priesthood being drawn to the civil rights struggle, being impressed by the War on Poverty and the Great Society, and becoming involved in the Vatican II reforms in the Church which expanded its pastoral reach to the alienated and suffering. The meaning of America has always been captured best for me in the words of Emma Lazarus inscribed on the Statue of Liberty:

> Give me your tired, your poor,
> Your huddled masses yearning to breathe free,
> The wretched refuse of your teeming shore,
> Send these, the homeless, tempest-tossed, to me.

The Church and society, interchangeably and together enriching each other, were to be the place of compassion and help for the suffering.

Father Henri Nouwen, Father Don McNeill, and Father Doug Morrison wrote an insightful book on compassion several years ago. They ask, "How does compassion manifest itself?" And they answer: in solidarity. How is compassion disciplined and learned? They answer: by voluntary displacement. How is compassion lived out in the light of the Gospel? They answer: in discipleship.

First of all, they say that compassion manifests itself in solidarity, the awareness of being part of the human family, the sense of being linked to other people, the profound conviction that all of us are joined together in the same human condition. We are more alike than different. As the Buddhist proverb put it: Though our skins may be of many different colors, our blood runs the same hue. Solidarity isn't just an intellectual affirmation of shared humanity; it is the deeply felt experience of human sameness. Unfortunately, we grow up in a world which teaches us all the many ways we are different from others—better, superior, more talented. The divorce experience can do the same thing by making one feel that no one else has ever suffered as I am suffering; no one else has ever known such pain, has ever had such fear, such uncertainty. Growing through the divorce experience should help me experience my bonds with other hurting divorced people, but should also draw me out in solidarity with all people who suffer. Support groups are schools of compassion when they help the divorcing discover that they are not alone, and are not the first person to walk this unsettling path amid a broken existence. The monk Thomas Merton prayed, "Thank God that I am *like* other men and women, that I am only a man among others . . . ." The compassionate divorced person is not the observer in the group but the participant, one who is willing to be vulnerable and not in control, one who moves from the fringe to the center of things rather than keeping at a safe distance, one who eventually reaches out to others who are in need.

How then do we make compassion more visible in our ministry and in our daily lives? Is there a method or a technique by which we can become more compassionate? Like being a Christian, compassion is a divine gift which is usually detected only after it has been acquired. It is probably best understood as a way of discipleship by which the gift is made visible and available. The three priests in their book on compassion say this is by way of displacement, that is, by unmasking the human illusion of having it all together and beginning to experience that we are all broken in need of healing. It means moving beyond all the restrictive norms of proper behavior, all the inherited rules which tell us how to behave properly in the face of upset, and learning to be with the unsettled in their pain, however awkward or uncomfortable that might seem. Without voluntary displacement a support group member may slip into the role of counselor or spiritual guru, protecting oneself by displaying one's knowledge and togetherness. There may be many forced tears but no real service. Displacement means being able to move with the hurting into places that threaten and challenge, new terrains of emotional upheaval, a world of threatening questions and doubts. Only such displacement and identification makes true Christian solidarity possible.

At this point one might begin to think that all this talk

about compassion is all well and good, but is it possible? Is it really possible to relate to one another's emotional burdens? In the face of our own emotional limitations and the gravity of others' problems, is this even realistic? The possibility of true compassion, the three priests say, only makes sense as an expression of discipleship. They write: "In the resurrected body of Christ, marked by the wounds of the cross, all human pains have entered into the center of the divine life. In Christ, God revealed himself to us as a compassionate God because in Christ he suffered fully with us and became fully present to us. Therefore, only of Christ can it be said that he knows what suffering is, that he really understands. Therefore, only of Christ can it be said that nothing human is alien to him and that there are no limits to his solidarity with the human condition. Therefore, only Christ, who did not sin, can be called compassionate in the fullest sense of that word."

When we talk about discipleship we are not talking about following Jesus as an example of compassion in some distant way; rather, it means that we realize that our compassion comes from Christ himself who, present in us, reaches out to heal his broken people. Just as the moon depends for its light on the sun, so all our compassion is dependent on God's compassion which comes to us in Jesus Christ. With Christ's strength, we bear the burdens of one another, and we learn that his yoke is easy and his burden is light. When joined to Christ's compassion, our acts of love and service are expanded and we are able to absorb a great deal of pain without becoming depressed. Genuine Christian compassion comes only from prayerful reliance on a God who has chosen to make his healing love present in the world through our embrace of one another. This dependence on God frees us and enables us to hang loose in the best sense; we need not fret about all the people to be reached and all the wounds to be healed, or worry about our every turn of phrase and every little gesture. If we are one with Christ in his solidarity and displacement, then the right words and the right gesture will (almost surprisingly) come out. We will begin to see that the deeper our relationship of discipleship with Christ, the deeper becomes our connection with those who suffer. Compassion means being one with the broken in solidarity, moving from the safe places to be with them, and prayerfully, easily, letting the compassion of Christ come through in our lives.

There are so many examples of this growth in compassion which I treasure from my years in this ministry. I remember Alice who grew through the pain of divorce, gave leadership to our Boston group, and then went off to Africa as a teacher. I recall Roni with a heart as big as the sky for divorced people, who went back to school and now works as a trained counselor with battered women. I think of Gerry who gave leadership to a local group and now works as an advocate with the marriage tribunal. There are so many more, who all underscore the potential for divorce ministry to be a school of compassion.

Generosity

One of the hallmarks of spiritual recovery after divorce is generosity. Diane taught me that. There is an ancient story, which she first shared with me, about an old monk in the desert which beautifully portrays a generous heart. This old monk lived in a hut in the desert several miles from town, and he would buy the little food he needed by weaving straw baskets and selling them in the town marketplace. One morning as he was heading into town with a few small baskets tied to his belt, he met an old cripple sitting by the road. The cripple spoke to him, "Holy Father, I must go to town to beg, but I have no one to take me. Please carry me." So the old man hoisted the cripple on his back and carried him to town. When they arrived he deposited him at the city gate where he spent the day begging.

The holy man sold his baskets, bought a few provisions, and had a few coins left over. As he was leaving the town, the cripple was still in the same place. "Holy Father, I have received nothing all day. Give me the coins you earned." The holy man gave him the coins. "Now carry me back where you found me; I have no one to help me." So again he hoisted the cripple on his back and carried him to the place where he had found him. As he put him down, the cripple said, "Holy Father, you are filled with divine blessings in heaven and on earth." As the holy man looked closely at him, he saw no man, but rather an angel of the Lord. In a moment, the angel vanished.

When I was a young priest working in Chicago, I met many

"gentlemen of the road" as we would call them, who would always ask a priest for a quarter for coffee. If I had a quarter in my pocket I always gave it to them, thinking to myself, "There but for the grace of God go I." One day I met a Catholic nurse who worked at a Salvation Army shelter for alcoholics. "You priests are the worst friends these alcoholic men have," she challenged me. "You salve your guilty consciences by giving them quarters, whereas you'd do a much better thing if you refused them any money and told them to shape up. A quarter's worth of booze is another nail in their coffins." I've never forgotten the truth she helped me see about false generosity.

Because of conscientious people like this nurse or stories we've seen on TV, most of us unfortunately have become overly suspicious of people looking for handouts. We wonder if they really have thousands in the bank or if they are slowly killing themselves. Sometimes people looking for handouts can be aggressive and obnoxious, trying to shame you into giving them something. In our modern cities it's easy to learn how to keep looking ahead, not to betray an emotion, and to keep on walking. We know too that giving people money can be a way of avoiding more significant involvement with them or a way of getting them out of sight quickly whatever the consequences for them may be.

Diane helped me see that the same kind of thing can happen to a person after divorce. She had been burned by an unfaithful spouse, judged harshly by family and friends, and made to feel like a "sinner" by "good people." "I erected a shell," she said, "an impenetrable coating which I hoped would protect me from more pain in the future. I got to.be like a turtle. I got myself back together, but the final product was fairly lifeless and pretty slow. I wasn't winning any races."

She told me that she was deeply touched by a homily I gave one Sunday on Zacchaeus the publican, a wonderful model of generosity. We remember how Zacchaeus, a small man and a tax collector, wanted to see Jesus when he was passing through

town, but he was short, so he climbed a tree to get a better view
of the Lord. Jesus surprised him by greeting him and inviting
himself to Zacchaeus' home for dinner. Zacchaeus was very
well-off, and we would guess that he threw a great party for Jesus and his friends. He was so impressed by the Lord that he
underwent a complete change of heart. "Behold, Lord, half of
my goods I give to the poor; and if I have defrauded anyone of
anything, I restore it fourfold." Jesus, deeply touched by Zacchaeus' turnaround and generous spirit, said, "Today salvation
has come to this house, since he also is a son of Abraham. For
the Son of Man came to seek and to save the lost" (Lk 19:1–10).

Zacchaeus, a wealthy man, freely detaches himself from
his goods and starts a new life. The story challenges those ties,
those creature comforts, those personal tastes which distance us
from the unattractive, the outcasts of our day. Zacchaeus reminds us that the material blessings we possess are there to free
us for service of God and neighbor, not to tie us to consumer
goods.

Once converted, Zacchaeus goes beyond the requirements
of the law in offering restitution. He *goes beyond*—a phrase
which challenges our own carefulness and guardedness. How
carefully do we measure our time, our talents, our interest in
others? How reluctant are we to just be with others, waste time
with them, stay with them in their time of trouble? Gospel generosity involves more than giving money. We see in the story of
Zacchaeus that it means going beyond our normal patterns and
giving more of ourselves to others.

Zacchaeus welcomes Jesus joyfully, demonstrating one of
St. Luke's favorite themes in his Gospel—that the following of
Jesus is marked by joy and festivity. Diane said she began to see
that these characteristics of Zacchaeus—detachment, going beyond, and joyfulness—were qualities that should mark the life of
a "recovered" divorced person. She began to see that she needed
a larger life perspective which would help her sort out her values

in her new life situation. Where is God in my life now? Where are people in my life now? Where are things in my life now? This perspective puts material things, material standards of success and material security all in their appropriate place, and sees that real living involves a certain "hang-loose" quality in relationship to things and a reorientation to God and people. "There are so many people around who would tell me to be careful, to be on guard, not to be too risky now that I'm divorced. The message that came home to me from the Zacchaeus story was that I needed to stretch myself beyond—to reach out deeply to new people, get in some new involvements, begin to dream about new possibilities for myself. A sad, hang-dog face on a divorced Catholic turtle is certainly no advertisement for a new life!" We talked about joyfulness and the fact that it must be worked at—we must reflect on God's abiding love and care, our own capacity to grow and change, the goodness of people who come into our lives—and learn to count our blessings.

On the recent anniversary of his ordination, a priest friend, Bob Kinast, wrote a poem about Zacchaeus:

> At first the tree was for a better view
> of the new movements
> filling the village of our expectations.
> But the view soon thickened into vision
> and beckoned to keep me aloft
> till a voice from the surging crowd
> inquired about dinner
> and what wealth I'd be willing to share.
> By now, I've learned that the art of priesting
> is to know when to dream and when to decide
> when to eat and when to feed
> when to climb the tree and when to throw the party.
> And always remember:
> pick a sycamore in the heart of town.

The divorce transition, as Diane began to understand, is an invitation from a God who cares about our future and invites us to change our hearts; he invites us to replace the wounded, bitter hearts with new hearts full of generosity, and, like Zacchaeus, throw a party.

"All this pain and heartache, all this anxiety and struggle, would have all been for nothing if I'd become one more tough, on my guard, self-protective person. The silver lining in this cloud has got to be the possibility that I am being stretched into becoming a more flexible, sensitive person. Yet the story of your Salvation Army nurse has taught me too, Father, that I can't simply give myself away. I have to take appropriate care of myself. I have to take care of my resources. I may even have to say 'No' to some requests which would be harmful for me or the person asking. Yet the more I've learned to 'go beyond,' the more I am able to comfortably say 'No' when necessary. True generosity, I've learned, is not buying friends or buying them off quickly, or even looking good. It's learning 'when to eat and when to feed— when to climb a tree and when to throw a party.' It's finding the generous balance that's at the heart of life, giving when the giving flows out of us like a river and giving too when the giving is very hard."

Generosity looks like the holy man in the desert. He had no great agenda, no great plans for himself or the world. He was free enough and attentive enough to see the cripple by the road. Yet he was unable to say "no" to the cripple's request for a lift into town. I'm sure he knew St. Paul well: "Bear one another's burdens and so you will fulfill the law of Christ." When the beggar asked for his few coins, he gave them to him readily; he had confidence in the God who had provided for him so far and would continue to do so in the future. When he places the cripple down, and sees in his place an angel, he must have thought of that lovely sentence from the Old Testament, "those who have welcomed strangers have often entertained angels unawares." The holy man found God not just in his little hut alone in prayer; he also found him in the cripple by the road.

I told Diane that it was for this reason I told the Salvation Army nurse, whom I admired greatly, that I would continue to give quarters to the men on the street. "I'll even buy Girl Scout cookies and put a coin in the Salvation Army Christmas kettle and buy some pencils from the blind man. I'm always afraid that if I don't do so I might miss the angel. There's always a risk that the angel will have horns, and that we'll be taken advantage of and made a fool of, but there's a greater risk that we might become suspicious and cold-hearted. We might miss the angel hiding in those old clothes or in that Girl Scout uniform, and, worse than that, we might miss the angel in ourselves."

Diane and I talked about my worry that sometimes our divorced Catholics ministry seems to be providing such picture-perfect models of recovery after divorce that we seem to be proposing nothing different from the secular ideal of the well-put-together man and woman. We may even be turning out good turtles. Divorced people who have undergone a real change of heart after the suffering of their divorce are certainly supposed to be humanly together people, but there's also supposed to be something special about them—something that the world in all its secular wisdom doesn't understand. It's that walking an extra mile, giving away the shirt off your back, turning the other cheek. Jesus said, "Go forth, and be poor in spirit, be meek and humble, be a comfort to others, be a seeker after justice, be merciful, be clean of heart, be a peacemaker, be willing to suffer for justice's sake. In a word, be generous."

Diane is today one of the most beautiful people I know—my favorite soft-shell turtle. She's got her act personally together, but there's something more about her, something beautiful—a generous heart.

Commitment

Kathy told me that she was really upset by a homily she heard at Mass on Holy Family Sunday. "All the priest talked about was marriage commitment," she said angrily. "The whole implication was that anyone who wasn't still in a first marriage was a bad Christian. What about all those people who are holding on like zombies in loveless marriages?"

"Easy," I said. "I didn't hear the homily; what he said obviously could have been expressed a little more sensitively for people like yourself, but what's wrong with speaking about commitment in marriage on Holy Family Sunday? After all, from what we know from the Gospels, didn't Mary and Joseph have just one marriage?" Kathy didn't look convinced. "Can I make a suggestion," I went on, "about why you possibly are so upset? It's something I've noticed in a number of my divorced friends. You become oversensitive to talk of commitment in marriage because your marriage commitment came apart. You shouldn't be. You are not an uncommitted person, Kathy. In fact, you strike me as a person of profound human and religious commitments. Just because your marriage didn't work doesn't mean you are not living a committed Christian life."

Kathy's anxiety about commitment is not unusual among divorced Catholics. They need to reflect upon commitment— not just marriage commitment, but more fundamental commitments to God, to others, and to oneself. It has struck me from talking with many divorced people that the shattering of their marriage commitment has raised doubts in many of them about their basic capacity to make commitments. I've met some divorced people adrift and lost, even some cynical, disillusioned and embittered. They say, "I'll never get involved again. I'll never get burned again."

Kathy and I got a cup of coffee and began to talk. There is no life without human commitments, I began. There is no healing after the trauma of divorce which does not involve making new commitments. There's no new life, single or remarried, which is not shaped by many new commitments.

In reshaping the commitments in one's life after divorce, I suggested that the committed life of Jesus presents a most helpful model. The central commitment of Jesus' life was to God, his Father. About him Jesus was unreserved in his love, his obedience, his trust, and his praise. His commitment was always total, but as we look closely at the Gospel pages we see that it was a commitment that developed and deepened during the final years of his life. His consciousness of his Father's love for him enabled him to see his Father's love everywhere—in the flight of ravens, in the lilies of the field, or in lepers who had been exiled from the town. He was relaxed and unself-conscious when he spoke about his Father. When his disciples asked him to teach them how to pray, he began warmly, intimately, "Our Father . . . ." The reason that his teaching and his insights always seemed fresher and deeper than others came from the fact that he was so close to, so much at peace with, his Father.

This bedrock commitment of Jesus to his Father flowed into commitments to others. He came close to those men and women who became his disciples, and he seems to have been very close to friends like Martha, Mary and Lazarus whose home he frequented. His commitment to God's people was wide-ranging. He reached out to young and old, rich and poor, the healthy and the sick, the prominent and the rejected. They sensed his love for them, and their devotion to him was evident from the love that went out from the crowds wherever he traveled.

His commitment to his Father and to his people did not tie him down; rather it freed him. He freely took on the burdens of those who came to him in pain. He reached out to touch the insane and diseased, to teach the ignorant and unbelieving, to lead home the lost and forgotten. His life reveals that there is no life without commitment, no real living without loving, no true freedom without bearing burdens. His commitment brought with it a freedom not *from* but *for* others. It drew him into communion, relationship, friendship with others. It was a costly communion, eventually forcing him to lay down his life for his friends. His is a life of complete self-donation, a life freely and completely given. "He who loses his life will find it" (Mk 8:35).

"I prayed, Father, for years for my marriage to work," Kathy said. "I asked God over and over for strength and perseverance. The more I prayed the more I saw it couldn't work. Yet I felt God leading me. I talked to counselor after counselor, priest after priest, and every time their advice was the same. For the sake of my kids, myself and even my husband, I had to make that dreadful decision to divorce. I'll never forget that day. I was afraid, but I felt God closer to me than ever. I knew I had to do it. I knew God would understand."

Not every divorced Catholic has come to the point of divorce as sure of God's loving presence as Kathy did. Yet in story after story I have listened to, I have heard men and women making a decision that was based on a commitment to God, and a commitment to their spouse, their kids, and themselves. That was certainly true of Kathy. For others, their spouse makes a decision to end the marriage against their will. For the Christian the commitment of marriage is not absolute. It sadly may be a faulty commitment, a mistaken commitment, a doomed commitment. Unfortunately many Catholics have mistakenly identified their commitment in marriage with their total commitment to God, believing that by breaking their commitment to their spouse, they have broken their commitment to God. Being married is a way of living out one's commitment to God and others and self, but there can come a moment when the marriage commitment will have to be ended if God is to be served, and if we are to live as Christians with one another.

Jesus' perfect love for his Father and his Father's perfect love for him is the model of all commitments. Our human commitments and especially our marriage commitments strain to imitate the commitment of Jesus. We have all known beautiful marriage relationships in which devoted husbands and wives in their commitment to each other have given us over a lifetime a powerful sign of Jesus' committed love. Christian history is full of many great men and women who have led committed married lives, and, thank God, there are a great many committed married people yet around us.

Still we all know many relationships in which love falters and dies, often due to no personal lack of effort on the part of the spouses. Some marriage relationships become over time loveless and even destructive. To remain in a commitment which is bringing harm and continuing stress at the risk of everyone's well-being is not fidelity; it may be fear. The decision to divorce and end a loveless, empty relationship may be a courageous act of fidelity to God. God, who is ever faithful to us, calls us to grow through even the death of a marriage commitment to find a new committed life. (The Church recognizes that many decisions to divorce were just such decisions of Christian courage when later it annuls such marriages.)

Learning to accept a decision to end a marriage which another has made may be an equivalent act of courage. One may have resisted divorce and have been willing to carry on in a troubled marriage, but now because of another's action a marriage has ended, a commitment has been shattered.

Kathy and I discussed the divorce transition as a time for shaping new commitments—first of all, to God. The new commitment here is shaped around failure, forgiveness and new life. We have to reaffirm our faith in a God who gives us the gift of freedom, and accordingly permits us to make some serious mistakes in life, but faithfully, through it all, calls us again and again to new commitments. Maybe it is those who know they are no longer perfect who really understand the richness of his mercy!

Second, there should be a commitment to former spouse and children. Many divorces are marked by acrimony and bitterness between spouses and a great deal of ambivalence and uncertainty. Kathy worried about these questions: "How do I continue to relate as a Christian to this person I can no longer live with as husband or wife? How do we maturely try to shape some kind of continuing relationship which tries to prevent a bad situation from getting worse? Can we possibly make things better than when we were married?" I told her that I have met people who insist that they and their former spouses get along better now than when they were married. Yet I know other cases where there is much emotional disturbance and bitterness from one side, and all the other partner can do is to try not to contribute more to the pain.

We talked about commitment to children taking on new shape after a divorce. Life together will never be the same for the children as it was; it will be much different, but it can be much better. Children will need to be given continuing access to both parents and assisted in reaffirming their commitments to both parents.

Kathy felt that the most difficult commitments to deal with are the ones that surface when a person begins to move beyond the failed marriage and to establish new friendships. "New friends provide essential support at this time, when one's old friendships have become strained by the separation. I've learned that it's essential for me to work at a new single identity, not dreaming of some new marriage which will make everything immediately better." Healing, we agreed, is linked to making new commitments; they may be new friends, people in need to whom one reaches out in service, people at work, neighbors or relatives. The worst thing a person can do at this time is drop out or go into an extended withdrawal. One's resources may seem drained, and fatigue may be one's continuing partner, but a new life marked by new personal commitments is essential.

"There is no human life, no Christian life which is not a committed life," I said to Kathy. "Treasure the commitments that endure in your life, mourn the ones that died, shape new ones, and remember that the Lord's commitment to each one of us is irrevocable." We've talked many times since about commitment, and it's always a challenging conversation. Each time I observe how the commitments in Kathy's life have deepened.

Belonging

Catcholic

"*F*ather, you see these dog tags I'm wearing. They were given me when I joined the Marines during the Korean War. I wore them for twenty years in the military, and have worn them ever since; I've never felt dressed without them. See what it says here on the corner: 'Catholic.' I didn't consider myself a Catholic for a long time; I didn't go to church for over ten years. I pretended I was nothing. I've been discovering lately that I'm still a Catholic—it's in my bones. Nothing has ever replaced it. It was this rotten divorce that made me appreciate that being a Catholic still meant so much to me."

You only had to look at that man's face to tell that he had lived and suffered. It was a strong, weatherbeaten face, lined with experience. The day he spoke to me at a divorced Catholics conference in Buffalo, New York and held up his dog tag, he was beaming. The word "Catholic" on his lips sat there with pride.

In the past ten years I've met thousands of divorced Catholics, and I've grown to appreciate, as never before, the meaning of being Catholic. In J. D. Salinger's novel *The Catcher in the Rye* the smart-alecky teenager, Holden Caulfield, is walking with a friend through Central Park in New York City and notices two nuns in their black habits. "Why is it," he asks, "that Catholics are always trying to figure out if other people are Catholics?" I'm sure we can all remember when we were kids wondering whether a new movie star was a Catholic or whether a ballplayer was a Catholic or whether the new kid down the block was a

Catholic. There was something special about being a Catholic. You had the sense of being part of a unique group of people with a unique history and a unique set of beliefs. After all yours was the one, true Church founded by Christ himself on St. Peter. Catholics didn't believe just anything they wanted, they believed the central truths taught by Jesus himself and handed down through his Church over the centuries. And it wasn't easy being a Catholic; you couldn't have it your own way. Among other things, Catholics didn't eat meat on Friday, they had to go to Mass on Sunday, they didn't divorce, and they believed the Pope was head of the Church. There were all kinds of Catholics— Poles, Italians, Irish, Germans—and they lived in different parts of town and held different kinds of jobs, but they were Catholics, and felt a special bond with one another.

Obviously much of that has changed in the last generation, and the Catholic Church seems to have lost much of its distinctiveness. Catholics now eat meat on Friday, don't fast from midnight before going to Communion, and even can get married with permission in Protestant churches. Even though much of the appearance of Catholicism has changed, its heart remains the same. That's what my divorced ex-Marine was talking about in Buffalo. The heart of Roman Catholic identity can be seen nowhere more clearly than in the lives of divorced Catholics. Divorced Catholics continue to tell us some of the best things about being Catholic.

Unfortunately, because we were not always helpful when they needed it, many divorced and remarried Catholics drifted away from the Church. In recent years, there have been a number of significant attempts to find them and bring them back to the Church community. "Welcome Home for Christmas" and "Welcome Home for Lent" and special parish outreach programs have surfaced many divorced Catholics eager to be restored to Catholic life. As we get to know them, we hear a familiar story. Even though they did not feel welcome in local Catholic churches and may even have felt excommunicated, most never stopped praying, most never stopped thinking of themselves as Catholics, and most never became anything else. If they were hospitalized, they signed in as Catholics. Through it all, again and again, they experienced God's presence in their lives—a sense of protection in times of danger, a sense of healing in times of sickness, a sense of support in times of sorrow. All the while they missed not being able to go to Church and receive the sacraments, but they lived the best life they were able. Their stories reveal the bedrock of Catholic identity—belief in a God who loves each one of us and never abandons us. "I always knew God understood," one woman told me. "It was the Church that didn't seem to understand."

Another thing we've learned from the divorced Catholics movement is that Catholics are very good at forming groups. There is something remarkable about the fact that over a thousand divorced Catholics groups now exist in the U.S. and Canada. There are some support groups in the Protestant and Jewish communities, but nothing near the number of groups for Catholics. That suggests that there has always been a strong group identity about Catholics which generates a strong sense of community; when divorced Catholics experience some sense of disaffection from the Church, the sense of community only seems to get stronger. Maybe it's the looseness and mobility of our very pluralistic modern society that reinforces the need to belong and have an identity, or possibly, on a deeper level, it comes from the age-old Catholic understanding that we all become part of the Church in baptism and that we are all bonded to one another by faith in Christ. Sunday Mass and Catholic schools and Catholic ways of praying and living have all strengthened that sense of belonging to God and belonging to one another. "I came into this meeting of divorced Catholics somewhat nervously; I didn't know anyone in the room; and yet after I sat there for a while and began to look around me and take in the faces and listen to what people were saying, I began to feel at home, as though I really belonged."

In recent years for every Catholic who has slipped away from the Church at the time of divorce, twice as many have stayed in and stood their ground. They may have experienced words or looks that suggested that they were bad Catholics, or that they were a disgrace to their Catholic upbringing, but they hung on, insisting, "We're Catholic. It's our Church too. We're not leaving, and we want the Church to help the divorced."

These are the men and women who understood from childhood that the Church of Jesus Christ is not the company of the perfect and the holy, but rather the Church of the flawed and the failed. The Catholic Church in the United States has always been a Church close to its people for better or worse, a collection of richly diverse parishes where immigrant people found help with everything from finding jobs to finding a place to live. Catholic priests have been close to their people, drawn from among them, at home in the parishes where often they grew up. It's always been a down-to-earth Church shaped by its people's culture and traditions. That's the spirit that I see surviving in the divorced Catholics I have met all over these two countries who have pioneered this new ministry; they assumed that Catholic history required such help.

Langdon Gilkey, a Protestant scholar at the University of Chicago, says that one of the most distinguishing features of Catholicism has always been its rationality. When all others may be losing their heads, Catholics have tended to think things through. Catholicism hands on a received wisdom coming from the Gospels and from the lived experience of millions of Christians over the centuries. There is no problem, however new or however complex, about which Catholic tradition does not have something to say.

Not that the tradition has answers for every contemporary problem, but in Catholic history we stay in touch with thoughtful men and women who have gone before us and have tackled related problems in the past; they give us road maps to help us confront in an authentic Christian manner difficult modern problems.

When I first started meeting with divorced Catholics at the Paulist Center in Boston in 1972, the group selected education as one of its four major goals. The group wanted to know what Jesus and the Church had to say about divorce and remarriage; they wanted to understand better the social and psychological adjustment divorced people go through; they wanted to understand the special needs of children and what child psychologists might suggest which could be helpful. Knowledge is power, they seemed to be saying, and the truth will set you free. Being Catholic had prepared them to appreciate that intellectual understanding can relieve anxiety and anger.

As the Boston group began to be flooded with people seeking help, I felt overwhelmed and had to draw some limits on my availability to see people. At a group planning meeting, I said to the six people present, "I've got to make it clear that I can't be available to offer one-on-one counseling to every divorced person who comes here looking for help." One of the founding mothers looked straight at me and said, "We don't need you to counsel divorced people. We'll take care of the hurting people. All we need you to be is a priest; we just want you to hear confessions for people who have been away, talk to those who need information about annulments, give an occasional talk on theology or Scripture, and most of all celebrate the Eucharist for us. We'll take care of the hurting people."

I look back on that scene with amusement now. My messianic pretensions were pretty quickly deflated by this woman's very Catholic sense that the Church was a community whose members should care for each other. They already had grasped the ministerial vision of the whole Church community which the bishops had taught at Vatican II: they knew that all the baptized were called to minister to one another in the Church. Their sense of Church wasn't a group dispensing easy spiritual remedies, but rather a Church of caring people, surrounding one another in time of threat, and comforting, supporting and healing each other.

A young Louisiana Baptist man whom I met at a support group in Lake Charles told me that this support group had prompted him to begin instructions to become a Catholic. I asked him why someone would move from a Protestant church in which the divorced could remarry to the Catholic Church whose teaching and rules on divorce and remarriage were much stricter. "I know it's harder, but you Catholics have something. When I got divorced, I thought God had abandoned me. I knew there was no way to get reconciled with my wife, so I stopped going to church. I felt guilty and punished. These divorced Catholics reached out to me, invited me to their meetings, and taught me about a God who loves us no matter what, forgives us our wrongs, and offers another chance. I've come to love again here. I like God again and I think he likes me. I just want more of it. That's why I want to become a Catholic."

Maybe that man said it all. There are many imperfections in the Catholic Church; many of its people and leaders do not always lead the most exemplary lives, and the Church does not always seem to be on top of many pressing issues. Yet at the grassroots, the life of the Church goes on, as it does in that support group in Lake Charles. There the people get together, tell their stories, share their faith, comfort and encourage one another. There God is present touching, healing, strengthening the suffering, drawing them to himself.

I always like to look at support groups as *ecclesiolas*, which is the Latin word for "little churches." Certainly on one level the Church is the Pope in Rome and the vast structure which links 600 million Catholics around the world. But at its base, the Church is built up of living stones, men and women gathering together in faith and love at the parish level, at the support group level, and there God is present among his people. "When two or three are gathered together, there I am in the midst of them."

It's not easy being a Catholic as my young friend from Lake Charles seemed to sense. But through all the wondrous complexity of such a vast Church, we find it continuing the work of the Lord at the grassroots, leading men and women home to him.

Church

"*F*ather, several years ago I went to hear you speak. I had never been to a meeting for divorced Catholics, and I found the whole experience exciting. All these new ideas, all these great people. When you were finished, people were lining up to speak with you; I got in the line, feeling that I had to speak with you. When it came my turn, I blurted out, 'Father, I married a drunk and a gambler, and have four children; I put him out three weeks ago. What should I do now?' I look back now and laugh, as if you were supposed to have some magic answer that was going to make everything turn out right for me. You put your arm around my shoulder and said, 'Have you found a support group yet?' I answered, 'Yes,' and then you said, 'Keep going to meetings.' "

I love that story, because many times people ask questions which make me think on my feet. I'm not always sure I have a good answer when put on the spot. But looking back, I like the advice I gave that woman. Join a group, get connected, find support, get ongoing help. When people ask me to define a support group, I tell them I could offer the definition which comes from the helping professions and which says that a support group is a gathering of people who ally themselves together to help one another deal with stressful life events or issues. Again, I prefer to suggest that a support group is a "little church," an *ecclesiola* in Latin. "Where two or three are gathered together, there I am in the midst of them." In a support group Christ is present to us in

162

a special, more powerful way because we bring him to each other. By sharing our lives with one another and sharing the ways we find God speaking to us in our experience, we help one another overcome personal subjectivity, blindness or narrowness; in a group the ways of God's presence among us are amplified and expanded. Our everyday words become the bearers of God's comfort and challenge to one another; our touch becomes the bearer of God's healing presence to one another.

Since the Second Vatican Council we Catholics have spent a great deal of time reflecting on the nature of the Church. One of the most helpful definitions of the Church I have found is one proposed by Father Richard McBrien of the University of Notre Dame. He begins by saying that the Church is "the community of believers who acknowledge the Lordship of Jesus." We Christians are men and women who are haunted by the memory of Jesus of Nazareth. The British historian Arnold Toynbee once said that Christians are people who look over all the great men and women of world history, examine everything they thought and proposed, and then come across this one man, Jesus of Nazareth, and say: Here's the one person who has put it all together; here's the one person who has understood the meaning of life; here's the one person who has shown us how to live.

At the heart of every effective divorced Catholics group is that central faith in Jesus of Nazareth, believing that he is the one who has helped us understand the meaning of suffering and rejection, who has helped us see that it is "in dying that we are born to life." We find in him a man who has known what it is to be fully human, and has experienced every aspect of our lives in greater intensity than we could imagine—every aspect except sin. Divorce ministry is not a ministry if it does not bring hurting men and women into contact with their Lord and help them acknowledge that he is for them "the way, the truth and the life."

Father McBrien goes on to say that this community of believers "ratifies that faith sacramentally." It is sometimes in-

sisted humorously that whenever two or three Catholics get
together they have Mass. There's something uniquely Catholic
about that impulse, for we believe that we do meet the Lord in
"the breaking of the bread and the sharing of the cup." We have
an instinct that the great truths that we are struggling to get into
our minds and hearts somehow come clearer and touch us more
deeply when we demonstrate them symbolically at the Eucharist. "As many grains of wheat make one bread, as many grapes
the wine, so we are all one body in Christ." The sacramental
symbols of bread and wine reveal bonds among us that speech
alone cannot describe. The dejected disciples, who did not understand the meaning of the Lord's suffering and death, met him
on the road to Emmaus and their hearts were on fire as this
stranger, whom they did not recognize, explained the Scriptures
to them about the suffering servant of Isaiah. It was when the
Lord sat with them at table and broke bread that they recognized
him. The breaking of bread helped them see that their broken
hearts and broken lives were but the same passageway for them
to faith-filled life as crucifixion and death had been for him. The
breaking of bread has helped Christians ever since understand
the relationship of the suffering of Christ to their own suffering.
"Unless the grain of wheat falls into the ground and dies, it remains only a seed; but if it dies, it sprouts up and bears fruit."
The Eucharist is an ongoing portrayal of God feeding and
strengthening his suffering people.

This is why divorced Catholics so hunger for the Eucharist;
they are drawn to these powerful words and actions, for they
mirror their own suffering and struggle. Every ongoing, vital divorced Catholics group I have known regularly celebrates the
Eucharist together, especially in one another's homes where the
celebration of word and sacrament can be so powerfully attuned
to the special spiritual needs of the divorced. I've met many people who told me that it was these small group Eucharists which

opened their eyes to the meaning of their Catholic faith for them.

In Father McBrien's view this community goes on to "commit itself to membership and mission." Divorced Catholics assert their place in the Catholic community and celebrate their belonging, deepened by the suffering they have endured. The divorced are especially important to the community because their witness of broken lives, healed and restored by faith, can be an important beacon to the rest of the community of the Lord's mercy. They tell the world that the community of Christ is a gathering of many people with many different life histories, with different levels of success and failure in living the Gospel, with varied resources and levels of commitment, all bearing one another up as brothers and sisters in Christ. Catholics are people with a mission, people on the move. They don't sit around and congratulate themselves for what they've seen and accomplished, but rather their eye is always looking out for the alienated, the disaffected, the lost. Like the Good Shepherd, who leaves the ninety-nine behind and goes off into the wild to find the one lost sheep, they leave the comfortable confines of the community and go into the world to invite others to belong and believe. There is a restless quality about this Christian community, as long as there is one person searching for love and hope.

All this is done, Father McBrien insists, for "the sake of God's Kingdom." All that we are about as God's people is to make his plan, his vision, his design for humankind take form here in human history. A support group, as a little Church, is itself a sign of the times to come. By the acceptance, mercy and love that divorced Catholics show for one another in their gatherings they show non-believers what God has in store for all people when his Kingdom comes. The Church of Jesus Christ strives to be an embodiment of the Kingdom to come, pointing to a coming era when there will be no more suffering, war, poverty and disease, a time when all people of all time will live together in justice, and peace, and harmony, a time when all will sit in peace at the Great Banquet and enjoy together the hundredfold that God has promised those who love him and each other.

A divorced Catholics group has a very concrete, modest, here-and-now purpose: to provide encouragement, help and support for men and women going through the heartbreak of divorce and working at piecing together a new life. Yet because they gather as Christians united in faith, their ministry to one another takes on a greater significance. Their little gathering is a cell in the body of Christ, the Church. Insofar as they love and heal one another and bring the sorrowing to new life, they renew and build up the whole Church. Insofar as the Church is built up in the world, and more and more men and women come to faith, God's design for humanity, his Kingdom, becomes ever more visible, ever more compelling.

Divorce ministry strives not to keep people in divorce support groups forever, but rather to renew and reshape them as Catholic believers, so that when their healing time has been accomplished, they may move back into the larger body of the faithful and assume larger roles of ministry among God's people. Divorce ministry has accomplished its goals if men and women come through this troubling transition stronger members of the community of believers, more deeply committed to Jesus Christ as one's personal Lord and Savior, ever watchful to reconcile the wavering and the scattered, living a life which worships God and celebrates his sacred actions among us, and helps others see beyond the torments and cares of life in this world to a new world to come which has already begun to take shape among us.

Membership

Often divorced Catholics are told that they're "out of the Church" because of what they've done, or Catholics who marry a second time without the Church's approval are told that they're excommunicated. Nothing could be farther from the truth. No matter what happens to the marriage of two Catholics, no matter how many times they get divorced or remarried, they remain Catholics. We know too well the serious spiritual and psychological damage done to divorced and remarried Catholics who were misinformed and felt that they were cast out of their religious home. The Church is working hard today to repair that damage and prevent further harm.

When I meet Catholics who believe that they are out of the Church because of divorce or remarriage, my first concern is always to assure them that through all their marital difficulties they never ceased being part of the Church. If they have been separated from the Church, I assured them that through all these years of alienation they remained part of the body of Christ, sharing in all our prayers for the people of the Church. Their good lives during this time of separation were building up the body of Christ. I always stress that we missed their presence, their gifts, the witness of their good lives. We've been the poorer without their participating in the life of the Church community.

When I ask them what it was like to live as a Christian without participating in the life of the Church, they always say it was tough. They missed Mass and the sacraments; they often felt envious of others who took these things so casually. Yet, almost without exception, they say they continued to pray; at some very beautiful times and at some very difficult times they experienced God's presence and his love. I'm always reminded in these situations of the words of St. Augustine, "Some who belong to Christ do not belong to the Church; some who belong to the Church do not belong to Christ."

One night I was speaking at a church in South Boston, and a man came up to me, smiled, and said, "Remember me?" Somewhat embarrassedly I replied, "I remember the face, but I can't remember exactly where we met."

"Well, Father, I went to confession to you two years ago at the Paulist Center, after having been away from the sacraments for almost twenty years since I got divorced. You said something that day that changed my life."

I asked rather intently, "What did I say?"

"You said, 'Welcome back.' "

Isn't it always the simple, human things we say which have the greatest impact? I'm sure I felt that day a great deal of sadness that this man had been needlessly away from the sacraments all these years, but I'm sure I also felt a great sense of joy that he had come home.

We're beginning to appreciate more these days that the Church is not just an institution; it's a home. A poet once said, "Home is where they have to take you in." The Church is the home of all the baptized, and they all always belong. Speaking in 1981 on the alienation of so many divorced and remarried Catholics from the Church, Pope John Paul II insisted that they always remain part of the Church because of their baptism. Nothing that happens in their marital histories erases their baptism. We may have so-called "bad Catholics," "lapsed Catholics," and "non-practicing Catholics," but they're all still Catholics.

The writer Joel Wells tells of a friend of his who thought because of disagreements he had with Church teaching he had left the Church four times in recent years, and every time he checked it out, he found out he was back in the Church. Even those Catholics who deny the faith, abandon their Catholic commitment and reject the Church are still in a sense a part of the household of the faith and a member of the Church. The Church teaches that baptism achieves a permanent effect, provided that some minimal dispositions are present in the recipient and the ceremony is properly performed by the minister of the sacrament. The Church reminds us that the sacraments are principally and foremost God's intervention in our lives, and that he holds us always in the palm of his hand, and he never forgets us. I have often found that alienated divorced Catholics are like wilted flowers; give them the refreshing water of some good pastoral care and they perk up quickly. The Church teaches that the sacrament of baptism is like that too; even if the recipient of a sacrament had little or no faith and even if he or she had lived a long time apart from the Church, baptism can revive when faith and Catholic life become more vital. It should be consoling to all of us to realize that the Catholic Church has always required very little in regard to human dispositions necessary to receive the sacraments effectively, and as a result requires minimal commitment necessary to remain a member in good standing. There's room for us all. As Father Jack Finnegan puts it: "Here comes everybody! The Church is a potpourri of saints and sinners, rich and poor and all varieties of the human condition as they join in the brotherhood and sisterhood of the Catholic faith."

A very important development has been underway in Catholic life since Vatican II. We are appreciating anew that Church membership is based on commitment and good works and a good life, not just on being baptized. Our contemporary parishes and our divorced Catholics groups present many important challenges for Catholics to perform the corporal works of mercy, function as responsible citizens, and develop a strong Christian spirituality. It is important that Catholic preaching, Catholic education and Catholic publishing all identify the criteria of excellence necessary to be a member of the Catholic community in the world and the broader Christian family. We know today that we cannot ignore the threat of nuclear war, worldwide famine, or the struggle for justice in our cities.

Still the Church must always show that mercy is a part of Christ's message, and never stress a teaching of Christ or the Church to such an extent that the community of believers is ill-prepared or unwilling to live with the imperfect response and accept those of minimal commitment. Certainly the divorced and the remarried have suffered here. The Church has always proposed and always will propose the teaching of Jesus that marriage is meant to be permanent and there should be no divorce; yet those who have been unable for whatever reason to live up to that teaching should not feel cast out from our midst. Our solidarity as God's people should always generate the compassionate posture, "There, but for the grace of God, go I."

The Church must do all it can to help people marry well and live happy married lives. We Catholics need not feel ashamed of our Church's efforts in this area. Look at the wide array of marriage preparation programs across the country, all the programs to support couples in marriage, and the great number of Catholic social service or Catholic counseling agencies, all undergirding our Catholic values about permanence in marriage. It is because those "upfront" ministries function so well in so many places, that the ministry to divorced Catholics is not seen as threatening to the Church's mission to support our traditional values in marriage. It may well be because of all these efforts that the Catholic divorce rate has been declining since 1981.

Divorce ministry is a healing ministry. When someone is

hurting and adrift, we must drop everything, and like the Good Shepherd leave the ninety-nine behind, and go immediately to help the one who is lost. If our efforts on behalf of divorced Catholics raise some questions in sincere people's minds about the basic teachings of the Church on marriage and divorce, we have to face those questions and point out to the questioners the vast commitment of the Church which supports those values. Yet we can't hesitate to help the divorced for fear some will misunderstand; we must take that risk if we are to be a Church which makes Christ's mercy concrete in the world. Jesus in his own ministry was often misunderstood and criticized for reaching out to the suffering. There is an inevitable tension in the Church community between permanence and compassion; if that tension is not being felt, we may not be faithfully following Christ.

Father Jack Finnegan says that we could build the Church's whole pastoral ministry upon that beautiful phrase of Isaiah the prophet, which St. Luke applied to the ministry of Jesus himself, "The bruised reed he shall not break, the smoking flax he shall not quench." "Ministry is, after all," Father Jack says, "caring for Christ's body and its members the way he has cared for us."

Eucharist

---

*R*alph said he never made a decision not to go to Mass anymore; he just made one excuse after another, one week after another, and before he knew it, he hadn't been to Mass in six months. When he realized how long it had been, he thought to himself: What's the point now? I'm getting divorced, and I can't go to Communion. Betty knew why she didn't go to Mass in her parish church anymore; she just couldn't stand going. She and her husband had worshiped together there for years; she went once by herself, and felt self-conscious and thought people were looking at her. Lee was told by a friend that she was excommunicated from the Church because she had gotten a divorce. Bill said he didn't feel worthy; after all, wasn't he a bad Catholic for getting a divorce?

We Catholics are a eucharistic people. From childhood onward, going to Mass and receiving Communion has been at the heart of our relationship to God. Lent or exam time or some time of decision often became a time for daily Mass and Communion. Communion for Catholics has always been a time of intimate closeness to God, a time for the most intense personal prayer, a moment of peace and quiet joy.

There has been much confusion and misunderstanding about divorced Catholics and the Eucharist. Divorced Catholics enjoy all the rights and privileges that come to any Catholic; divorce in no way alters one's place in the Catholic community nor does it interfere with one's access to the Eucharist. In the United States we did have a penalty of excommunication attached to a second marriage "outside the Church." That law which was written by the American bishops in 1884 as a response to the early American divorce laws was removed in 1977. There is no longer any penalty in law which excludes the divorced and remarried from the Eucharist. Furthermore, the Church does not teach that divorce is a sin or that the divorced are sinners. Many sincere Catholics only make decisions to divorce after lengthy consultations with priests, spiritual directors and counselors. That's not to say that an individual may not do something sinful at the time of divorce, such as injuring a former spouse or refusing to provide support for children, but civil divorce itself is not a sin.

Once it becomes clear that the divorced who have not remarried are not excluded from the Eucharist because of law or sin, we are left with the deeper, more pervasive reason why so many drift away from the Eucharist. Many find themselves unworthy, or consider themselves people who have gone against God's plan and may be on the outs with him, or feel that God is angry with them. It may be that the divorce experience is so full of self-doubt and lessening self-worth that one almost automatically thinks the worst about oneself on all levels. Furthermore, at the time of separation and divorce, many people just drop out; they no longer mix with friends, give up their bridge game, feel unwelcome in Church activities. They don't feel they fit in anymore.

At the heart of this alienation from the Eucharist is also a serious misunderstanding about the Eucharist. Many of us were raised as children to think that the Eucharist was for very good people, those who had their acts together, those who deserved a gold star for keeping all the rules perfectly. The Eucharist was seen in this view as a reward for doing good. "Here I am separated and getting divorced. I've made a real mess of my life. I'm full of all this anger, bitterness and resentment. I'm especially angry at God. How could I ever go to Communion?"

The Church has been deepening its understanding of the Eucharist over the past twenty years in ways that have important implications for divorced people. We've all been aware of many changes in the Mass since the Second Vatican Council. Gone is the Latin, the altar against the wall, the hushed tones at Mass, the prayerful passivity in the pew. In less than a generation, we've grown to love the vitality of our Eucharist celebrations today—the joyful music, the ease of responding in English, the warmer sense of community around the table, the livelier feeling of God's presence in his word, in the sacrament, in his people. All this change has come about, not just because we wanted the people to participate better at Mass, but because we've begun to understand better what the Eucharist is all about.

When we gather to celebrate the Lord's Supper, we are drawn back to that meal which Jesus celebrated with his friends on the night before he died. We are drawn back as well to many other meals which Jesus shared during his ministry—meals which the Gospel writers saw as preparing for and giving meaning to the later Eucharist. It's clear from the Gospels that Jesus used meals often in his ministry to explain his mission. In the second chapter of the Gospel of Mark we read about Jesus calling Matthew, the tax collector, to follow him and become his disciple. Matthew is overjoyed and invites Jesus to dine at his home with his friends. Some of the "good" people in town did not like Matthew's friends, many of whom were Jews who didn't observe the law, or Jews who had intermarried with pagans, or tax-collectors. The "good" people considered them all "sinners." When Jesus heard them murmuring about the meal and the people with whom he was eating, he said, "It's not the healthy who need the physician but the sick; it's to search out and save those who are lost that I have come."

From the dawn of human history, people have always gathered together at meals, not just to satisfy their bodily hunger, but more so to satisfy their spiritual hunger. We've all eaten alone at one time or another; we know what it's like. The prospect of eating alone for the rest of our lives at a corner table at McDonald's is a fairly bleak prospect. When we dine with loved ones, relatives, friends, and even new acquaintances, our spirit is fed as well as our body. The best meals are marked by laughter and sharing good feelings. When we invite friends to our homes for dinner, they feel honored; when we haven't seen someone for a long time, a meal together is a great way of catching up. Jesus drew upon all these aspects of meals in his ministry. He used meals especially to show his love and acceptance for people who had been ignored, rejected, or cast out. He drew them to himself at table as a way of demonstrating the reconciling love his Father has for all people, especially those whom others thought did not belong.

When the disciples of Jesus wrote down the story of the loaves and fishes some forty years after his death, they used it to teach us something very important about the Eucharist. We read that thousands of people had been following Jesus for days, listening to his every word. "I have compassion on the people, because they have been with me now three days, and have nothing to eat, and if I send them away hungry to their homes, they will faint on the way; and some of them have come a long way" (Mk 8:1–10). When Jesus finds out that they have only a few loaves and some small fish, he commands them to have the people sit on the grass. "He took the seven loaves, and, having given thanks, he broke them and gave them to his disciples to set before the people."

Notice how similar the preceding words are to the words we hear so often at Mass: "On the night he was betrayed, he took bread, blessed and broke it, and gave it to his disciples." Here is Mark giving meaning to the Eucharist, suggesting that the Lord

we meet at Mass is the same compassionate, merciful Lord who
fed the thousands. His bread is food for the many, especially the
tired and the hungry.

Remember too the story of Zacchaeus, the short tax collector, who wasn't able to see Jesus because of the crowd, and
climbed a tree to get a better look. When Jesus sees him, he calls
out, "Come down, Zacchaeus. Tonight I want to dine in your
house." Zacchaeus is overjoyed, and invites all his friends, and
lays out a great dinner. In the course of the meal, Zacchaeus is
so impressed by Jesus that he experiences a complete change of
heart. "Lord, half of my goods I give to the poor, and if I have defrauded anyone of anything, I restore it four times over." The
meals of Jesus are times when flawed people find the capacity to
change their lives and begin to live as new people. Being with Jesus at table challenges the way we live.

The Eucharist we celebrate together draws us back in time
to that Last Supper which Jesus celebrated with his disciples on
the night before he died, but it also draws us ahead to that great
banquet at the end of time when all humankind will be gathered
at the heavenly table of the Lord. Jesus talked about that heavenly table in his ministry, and as usual he talked about it by telling a story. He told about a man who invited all his friends to a
great banquet, but when the time came, one by one they found
excuses not to come. The man was furious at the rudeness of his
guests, so he sent his servants out quickly into the streets and
lanes of the city to bring in the poor and maimed and blind and
lame. This story teaches that it's not the so-called "good people,"
the self-righteous, the condemnatory, who will have the first
seats at the banquet in the Kingdom of God, but rather the suffering, the despised, the poor, and the rejected.

That story and all these stories challenge our Sunday celebrations. Do the suffering, the rejected, the alienated feel welcome at our Eucharists? Does the warmth of our gathering
communicate compassion and acceptance? Does the preaching

invite the hurting to come find healing from the divine physician? Is the Eucharist presented as nourishment for the hungry, the struggling, the imperfect?

We've moved a lot of furniture around in our Catholic churches these past twenty years, and we've made a lot of stylistic changes in the way we celebrate the Eucharist. But have we communicated the fundamental message which is at the heart of the Vatican II reform? If the alienation of so many divorced Catholics from the Eucharist is any indication, we have not succeeded yet in bringing the "poor and maimed and blind and lame" to his table.

The Eucharist is not a gold star for winners. We all come to Eucharist as underachievers. Which one of us would dare stand in church on Sunday morning and tell God about our achievements? We all gather in our weakness and mediocrity and failure in search of reconciliation and healing. The Church teaches today that the Eucharist is primarily a sacrament of reconciliation. It is at the table of the Lord that we meet the divine physician offering us the necessary strength to keep going and to make it through another week. All he asks is what he asked of Matthew and Zacchaeus—that we come to him with an open heart, ready to root out of our lives everything that keeps us from loving and living at peace.

Our Eucharists have missed the divorced. We Catholics have been having a banquet with many important empty seats. We need these faithful men and women who have struggled through the heartbreak of a broken marriage and have begun to fashion a more mature, more realistic Catholic life. At the inn of Emmaus the two weary, disheartened disciples broke bread with a stimulating stranger, and they recognized him in the breaking of the bread. We all come to the Lord's table in our brokenness and recognize him, who was broken for us, offering us healing and reconciliation.

"What's all this talk about divorced Catholics being ministers to one another, Father? Aren't only Protestants ministers? I never heard about Catholics being ministers." Ben, a gray-haired man in his fifties, put that question to me at a conference in California. I asked him and the assembled group if they remembered the diagram of the Catholic Church which was found in our childhood catechisms. It showed the Church as a large triangle. At the top was the Pope, then under him the cardinals, archbishops, bishops, priests, sisters, and brothers, and, at the bottom, the lay people. The whole group remembered it well. I went on to explain that when the bishops of the world came together in Rome for the Second Vatican Council from 1962–65, they wanted to issue a statement about the Church. An advance draft had been prepared which basically described the old pyramid model. The bishops said that although it was true in a sense, there was much more to the Church than the pyramid portrayed. After much discussion, the bishops issued a new statement which said that the Church is, first of all, God's people. By baptism we all become members of that people, and we all receive roles and responsibilities in the Church. All of us by baptism are called to be like Christ in the world, and all of us are called to carry on his ministry of love and service in the world. All of us are called to minister.

Now there certainly are some men and women in the Church, I went on, like myself in whom the Church has invested a lot of time, money and effort in preparing for ministry. But I was a Church minister before I was ordained to minister in a special way as a priest. When I was called to priesthood by the bishop, I was called to a new order or level of service, called to work alongside, not apart from, all the baptized. We read in the Gospels that Jesus made himself the servant of all, washing the feet of his disciples, laying down his life for his friends. To become a priest, a bishop, or even the Pope is not to be promoted or raised up in the Church, but rather to take on a position of ever more demanding service undergirding, supporting and reinforcing the ministry of the whole baptized community. The Constitution on the Church of Vatican II really turned our old notions of Church upside down; in fact, it may have turned that catechism pyramid upside down. We now see better that the Church is God's people sent to live the Gospel in the world, supported by their priests, and bishops, and, ultimately, by the servant of the servants of God, the Holy Father himself. The Church can be faithful to its mission and effective in the world only when all members of the Church are fulfilling their appropriate ministerial roles with fidelity and integrity. Some are parents, some workers, some artists, some retired, yet all minister in their own life situations.

So, we agreed, all baptized Christians are called to minister in the world. I mentioned to that California group that I had to spend many years in a seminary preparing to be a priestly minister. Then I asked: "What school do lay people go to in order to prepare for their ministry?" (No audience has ever failed me when I ask that question.) They replied almost as if rehearsed, "The school of hard knocks." Life itself, all that transpires along our journey in helping us become the men and women that we are, all this has been part of our preparation for ministry. St. Augustine liked to quote St. Paul: "All things work together unto the good of those who love God." And St. Augustine would add, " . . . even their sins."

There's an old Portuguese proverb which makes the same point: "God writes straight with crooked lines." Everything that has happened to us in some way helps us minister better, even our divorces.

That's what we see happening in divorced Catholics groups where divorced people reach out to help each other. The learning, the expertise that the divorced bring to their ministry is the insight, the hard-earned wisdom, the spiritual depth which has come from their own struggle to grow through the heartbreak of divorce. When they touch a sobbing person's arm and say, "I know just how you feel," that means something, because they've been there. When a mother of four tells how she managed to raise those kids alone since her husband left, her practical insights mean something. When a middle-aged man talks about coping with loneliness and learning to make new friends, it means something. Divorce groups bring these people together to minister to each other, to share, to tell their stories, to befriend each other, to help others see in them the tenderness and mercy of God.

Divorced Catholics groups are more than psychological self-help groups. They are truly a ministry. Mel Krantzler once observed that he had seen lots of divorce adjustment groups, and the central issue always seemed to be: once you've given those divorcing all this information and support, how do you get them to believe in themselves again, how do you get them to pick up and begin to live again? "Your groups seem to be doing that," he said to me. "How do you explain it?" I told him that he had just touched what I considered the basic religious dimension of our groups, why we call this a Church ministry. We try to help people see that in the depth of their pain and loss, they meet a God who loves them and cares for them. They meet that God and experience him in the loving generosity of other people in the group. The group uses the traditional symbols of religion—the healing words of Christ, bread blessed and broken, the passage of Christ through death to resurrection—to help enkindle hope in the hearts of these doubting men and women. I always insist that there are many helpful, valid insights from psychology and all the behavioral sciences that help us understand the nature of grief and the expectable transitions people go through, but it is the spark of faith, the sense of not being alone but rather being loved by others and by God, the contagious hope that spreads from one to another—all this, open, named, spoken, shared, that makes gatherings of the divorced not just a mutual help group but a ministry.

Some among support group members are called to special ministerial positions of leadership. These can be demanding roles which require continuing support and nourishment for one's own journey, while reaching out to the recently hurting. The tasks of keeping a group going, welcoming newcomers, organizing a program, providing socials, dealing with the dissatisfied—all these can wear down quickly men and women in leadership. I challenge groups to be good to their leaders, and I also challenge leaders to take on only what is realistic. They need to develop good support for themselves by sharing tasks with others, and they need to provide for regular turnover in leadership. A good steering committee, whose members and chairpersons serve for about six months to a year at a time, seems to be a familiar structure in many successful groups.

It's important for people to know when it's time to move on. Some wonderful people stay with groups for years and find real personal fulfillment in ministering to others; they seem to get better at it as time goes on. They don't seem to need to control but consistently, quietly serve. Others look back on a period of intense and rewarding involvement in a group, but admit that they had to move on. They had to put the pain behind them; they couldn't keep talking about it. In many cases they moved on to other forms of ministry. The gift for ministry which blossomed in the context of the divorce group now finds wider range. I know divorced Catholics who have become active in social justice ministries, soup kitchens, reading to the blind, teaching in prisons, visiting shut-ins, teaching religious education classes to children, and a whole range of parish ministries. Nothing pleases me more than to see these new forms of service which recovery from divorce generates.

Gray-haired Ben didn't know he was a minister, but from what I learned, it was clear he was. He had never been anointed or prayed over, but helping others flowed naturally out of his basic Christian identity. That quiet, effective, almost unnoticed service of one another may be the finest ministry of all.

Priests

A chill had set in, as happens most late summer nights at Lake George in upstate New York's Adirondack Mountains. I came inside from the porch of the Paulist Fathers' summer house by the lake where I had been reading, and found Father Jim Walsh sitting by the fire wrapped in a blanket.

"How are things going with the ministry to the divorced?" he inquired as he looked up from a book.

"We're reaching a lot of people," I responded. "I wish divorce ministry didn't have so many people to reach."

Father Walsh, a gentle priest in his early seventies, then spoke about the divorced Catholics group at St. Paul's parish in Greensboro, North Carolina, where he is associate pastor.

"They're a very impressive group of people, and they make a tremendous contribution to the parish. They've been through so much; your heart really goes out to them."

We talked on about some other Paulists we knew who were working with the divorced. "There's a new pastoral approach emerging among priests generally," I said. "Where we used to find at best silence and at worst edicts of excommunication, we now find priests reaching out and reconciling people. I think we've begun to stem the loss to the Church of so many of the divorced. The best pastoral instincts of priests are coming to the fore."

"I look back sadly on the days we used to excommunicate

the second married and turn them away from the Church," Father Walsh said. "Many of us of my generation thought that was what we had to do. They had broken the Church's law and there was no other choice. We were very strict then; we felt we were bound to be. The happiest years of my priesthood have been these last fifteen years since the Council; I am so pleased that we don't have to turn people away, and that we can help them the way we're helping the people at St. Paul's."

That conversation captured so well for me the tension that so many American priests experienced for years, and why divorced Catholics found so many of them rigid and insensitive in their time of need. Seminary education before the Second Vatican Council trained these men to present clearly the teachings of the Church, and then forcefully to call the people to obey the Church's discipline. St. Alphonsus Ligouri, the great Church reformer, had advised priests to be "lions in the pulpit, but lambs in the confessional." Unfortunately many priests didn't have the necessary resilience and flexibility to fulfill that mandate, and many came through as thoroughgoing lions.

The American Catholic Church has always stood squarely in support of the family. Catholic parishes across this country historically welcomed great throngs of immigrants, many of them dislocated and broken families, and pastors marshaled all their physical and spiritual resources to protect and defend the sanctity of marriage. In the immigrant era, Catholic parishes provided people with homes, food, clothing, and even jobs. Catholic charitable organizations, orphanages, and parochial schools are all monuments to the Church's concern for the stability and integrity of family life. The temperance movement, the labor movement, and the many efforts at social reform led by Catholics all had as their major aim the protection of the family in a hostile society. The 1884 law which attached an excommunication to a second marriage "outside the Church" was not in its time a response to divorce among Catholics; very few of them were divorcing then. It was a response to a number of new civil divorce laws which were making divorce easier to obtain and were seen as threatening the family. The American bishops passed the law to make an important social and religious statement about the Catholic teaching on the permanence of marriage and its consistent stand against divorce.

American culture has always been harsh on people who failed. We're a nation that has always prized success, and we know of no worse "put-down" than to call someone a "loser." Condemnatory and rejecting attitudes toward the divorced and remarried have always been as American as apple pie, and have always been part of the religious climate of all the American churches. People who divorced were seen not only hurting their families, but hurting the whole society. It's not surprising then that our priest leaders over many generations insisted upon permanence in marriage and had little sympathy for the few who divorced.

Not that all priests were rigid and unyielding. A priest in northern Maine once told me that when he came to his first priestly assignment forty years before, he was sent to work under an eighty year old pastor. This old priest was loved by his people, and everyone in town, even non-Catholics, came to him for advice. "When I die and come before the judgment seat of God," the old priest once told him, "there may be only one thing the Lord will hold against me. He may say I was too easy. If he does, I think I'll be ready to give him an argument."

The Catholic Church in the United States would not be a vital religious community today if most of its priests over the years had not been close to their people and ministered effectively to them in all their trials and sufferings. Today ministering to the divorced and the divorced/remarried demands new pastoral skills and sensitivity that every priest does not possess. I was ordained sixteen years ago and hardly heard the word divorce in my seminary years. We studied the law of the Church on marriage, but gave no consideration to the personal and spiritual needs of people who divorce.

Consequently, when I first got involved in divorce ministry in 1972, I knew little about divorce and remarriage. I had much to learn about the history of the Church's teaching on marriage and the development of its laws and procedures. I had to learn about the psychological and social crisis that divorced people go through. I had to understand the painful spiritual crisis they go through, and the doubts and fears that confuse their relationship with God and the Church. I had to get on top of the reforming movements in the Church, legally, theologically, and pastorally, that were beginning to provide hope for the divorced and remarried. These were hard lessons to come by because so little was written or taught then on these very complicated issues.

Today when I give workshops to priests, I always like to introduce myself not as an expert on divorce but rather as a fellow pastor. I like to insist that everything I've learned about this topic has come from my own experience in the field and my desire to learn how to minister effectively to divorced people—and all of it has been post-ordination learning. (Even today many seminaries still do not have good courses to prepare the priests of the future for this ministry.) I have given study days in dozens of dioceses all across the United States and Canada, and I find the priests who attend almost unanimously searching for insights and practical approaches which can help them minister more effectively. This current generation of priests, men of all ages and backgrounds, are as serious today about helping their people as the priests of previous generations were in helping the immigrant people of their day.

When people tell me that their parish priest has seemed harsh or insensitive to the divorced in his sermons or at parish meetings, I always ask them if they've tried to talk with him. I suggest that they get a few of the divorced parishioners together and invite the priest over to one of their homes for coffee. Tell him, I suggest, that you would like to share with him what it's been like to be divorced in this parish. Most priests will then ask for help in making their language and actions more nuanced and sensitive. (One small group of divorced people succeeded at such a meeting in having the family picnic changed to the parish picnic with a clearer invitation for widowed, divorced and single people to attend.) My experience is that over a leisurely conversation they will admit that they feel great tension as a priest around these issues. How do they remain faithful to the Church's teaching on the permanence of marriage, while at the same time being kind to the divorced, without creating confusion in the minds of the parish about where the Church really stands? This conflict is very real for most priests, and not easy to work through.

The Church's responsibility to preach in season and out, the teaching of the Lord on the permanence and indissolubility of marriage is borne primarily by the teaching office of the Church, its educational institutions, and the array of programs which prepare couples for marriage and support those already married. In every parish those ministries should be encouraged, and the traditional teaching clearly preached. However, that traditional teaching should never be stated in such a way that makes the divorced feel that they are not good Catholics or that they do not belong in the Church community. The Lord in his own ministry called his followers to faithful commitments in marriage, yet reached out to the divorced. Priests who are in regular dialogue with both the married and the divorced seem to be able to strike the necessary pastoral balance which enables them to support both the value of permanence and the value of compassion. The divorced have to be willing to minister to their priests, as well as expect ministry in return.

"I never could have made it through my divorce without Father Smith," a woman once told me.

"What did Father Smith do for you?" I asked.

"Whenever the going got very tough, when it seemed that I was ready to boil over or go down for the third time, I would call him up and go over and talk with him."

"What did he say to you?" I asked.

"Well, I would just pour my heart out, dump all my anger and feelings on him, and talk on and on."

"What did he say?"

She thought for a minute. "Well, he said very little. In fact, I don't remember anything he said in particular. But he was always there ready to listen."

Father Smith is one of my heroes in divorce ministry. He gets an "A" from me. I sense that he recognized that there was little he could say at this time which would take away this woman's anger and upset. She had to work it through. He was willing to be an ally, be present, be there for her. That was a lot, and from what I could tell, it made all the difference.

Bishops

At a divorced Catholics conference in Indianapolis two years ago, Archbishop Edward O'Meara introduced me. "Father Young and I have a mutual priest friend, who tells me that Father Young has a thesis that the bishops in the United States who are most favorable to divorced Catholics ministry are those bishops who have had someone divorced in their immediate families. I think he's right. I never appreciated all the pain and confusion that follows upon a divorce for Catholics until someone in my own family recently got a divorce. I learned a lot."

The Church's ministry to separated, divorced and remarried Catholics has been a grassroots phenomenon in the United States and Canada, with divorced people themselves taking the initiative to reach out and minister to one another. Where their efforts have met the warm support of their local bishop, the ministry has flourished. It is a given of the Roman Catholic Church that the local church is pastorally led by the bishop as teacher and shepherd; if the bishop gives his support and leadership to a cause, then the rest of the Church community is much more likely to follow. We've been blessed in recent years in these two North American nations with many dedicated, pastoral bishops who have promoted this ministry and fostered its development.

In the early 1970's the American Catholic bishops proposed that the Catholic observance of the U.S. Bicentennial in 1976 should have two parts: a eucharistic congress in Philadelphia and a national symposium on justice in Detroit. The symposium would examine justice in the life of the nation and the Church and would be called "Liberty and Justice for All." I was fortunate to participate in both parts of the observance. I was invited to give a presentation on the Church's ministry to divorced Catholics at the Family Day of the eucharistic congress and was one of the principal concelebrants of the stadium liturgy celebrated by Cardinal Cooke. (I grew up in Philadelphia and have always been a Phillies fan; that night was the first time I ever made it to second base at Veterans Stadium.)

To prepare for the justice symposium in Detroit the bishops held surveys and hearings around the country to discover what were the justice issues on American Catholics' minds. Where in Church and society did they find liberty and justice for all still lacking? The issues and feelings that surfaced were sorted out into eight categories, one of them issues affecting family life. An enormous amount of grassroots feeling surfaced around the country suggesting that the Church should be doing more to help divorced Catholics. The bishops appointed eight committees to sort out the material submitted and come up with an action agenda for the Church so that it could become a better instrument of justice. Because of the large amount of interest in ministry to divorced Catholics, I was asked to serve on the family committee.

The committee was composed mostly of active lay people in family ministry and was chaired by Bishop Thomas Grady of Orlando, Florida. After much discussion we came up with a first round of suggested resolutions to be approved first by the convocation in Detroit and then be submitted to the bishops as a whole; I made the case in our committee meetings that the most significant single step the bishops could take at this time to effect the reconciliation of divorced and divorced/remarried Catholics to the Church would be to remove the 1884 American law which attached an excommunication to a second marriage "out-

side the Church." I argued that this law had become deeply internalized by American Catholics, and was at the heart of
attitudes which caused alienation of the divorced and remarried.
Since it was a law approved by the bishops in the nineteenth
century at a national meeting of the U.S. bishops, it would seem
to me that it was in their power to take this step toward reconciliation.

Bishop Grady did not respond at our first meeting, but
when we returned about three months later, he said that he had
thought about the removal of the excommunication when he got
home, and called up his old friend, Bishop Cletus O'Donnell of
Madison, Wisconsin, the chairman of the Bishops' Committee
on Canonical Affairs. Bishop O'Donnell said immediately,
"Let's remove it. It's bad law." So Bishop Grady suggested that
we include a resolution for removal of the excommunication
among our proposals.

When some 900 bishops, priests, sisters and laity from all
over the country gathered in Detroit in October 1976 to consider
a large package of resolutions on many aspects of Church life,
the family resolutions were the first presented to them. The
family resolutions, including five on the Church's ministry to
the divorced, were enthusiastically endorsed by the whole body.
It was a thrilling moment, but that's not the end of the story.
The resolutions passed were recommendations to the bishops for
action. The next step might be more difficult. Enter Bishop
James Hickey of Cleveland, Chairman of the Bishops' Committee on Pastoral Practices, and a real friend of the divorced.
Bishop Hickey's committee was given responsibility for studying
the recommendation on the removal of the excommunication.
He argued that this action was in keeping with the spirit of the
Second Vatican Council, and such action had been proposed by
Pope Paul VI in his letter implementing the decrees of the
Council. The Pope had called for local bishops to remove all excommunications which were stricter than the universal law of

the Church and which were not in keeping with the pastoral outreach of the Council.

Bishop Hickey argued to his brother bishops that such an action should be seen as a gesture of pastoral care and appropriate solicitude for the divorced and remarried, assuring them that they remained part of the Church and part of the Church's pastoral concern. The bishops voted 263–8 to remove the excommunication, and in November 1977 Pope Paul approved their action. This action was a watershed event for the American Church, representing a significant shift in posture. No longer were the divorced and remarried to be penalized and placed outside the community of the faithful, but rather they were to be cared for as brothers and sisters in need of help. No longer could the remarried and even the divorced be rejected as outside the pastoral concern of the Church.

"I have the pleasure today of introducing Father Young to speak to us about this most important matter. It's one that I, like all of us in the Church, need to understand better. All of us need to grow in appreciation of the suffering of the divorced. Now that I've introduced him, I want to sit down and learn myself." Archbishop Rembert Weakland, O.S.B., archbishop of Milwaukee, said that at a 1980 clergy conference there. His introduction captured a remarkable aspect of the ministry of so many of our bishops today—their willingness to admit they don't know everything, and an open recognition that they need to mingle among their people and learn.

In 1976 I was teaching summer school at Seattle University, and Roni Bissett, who was chairperson of the local divorce group, invited Archbishop Raymond Hunthausen, me and about a dozen divorced Catholics to dinner at her home. As we sat around sipping coffee after dinner, a woman from the group said to the archbishop: "We're having a difficult problem with our group and would like to ask your advice."

"Surely. I'll be happy to help if I can."

"Well, we have a man who is vice-president of our group, and he's getting remarried next week outside the Church. We've asked him to step aside as an officer of our group, since we have a ground rule that all our officers have to be in good standing with the Church. He doesn't want to step down, and feels that he should be allowed to continue in his position. We don't know what to do."

"Well, I'd like to see you work out that one yourselves. Don't you think you could talk it over some more and come up with a solution? By the way, I can see why he doesn't want to leave your group. You're such a wonderful group of people. Maybe he feels he needs your support all the more now that he's getting remarried."

"But, archbishop, we wouldn't want to do anything that would make our group lose your approval."

The archbishop smiled. "I think it would be very hard for your group to lose my approval. In fact, you don't need my approval to get together as divorced persons to help each other. The charity you offer to one another is not something the archbishop has to permit. Hopefully, that comes out of your basic Christian faith."

"But, Archbishop, we want your approval, because, after all, you're the Church."

Archbishop Hunthausen quickly replied, "No, you're the Church, and I have the documents of Vatican II to prove it."

I love that story, because most divorced and remarried Catholics in this country have not often heard archbishops tell them that they're the Church. But, of course, they are. They may be, as one bishop suggested recently, a new form of the Church suffering, and their sufferings help build up the body of the Church.

"I've come to share your pain," Pope John Paul II said to the people of Central America when he began his pastoral visit there in the late winter of 1983. Bishop Thomas Grady repeated those words at the concluding liturgy of a statewide Divorced Catholics Conference in Orlando a month later. That expression of solidarity in suffering with divorced Catholics captures for me the dramatic change that has occurred among our bishops these past ten years. At first, like most of us, divorce among Catholics made bishops very nervous; they worried about the Church's teaching on the permanence of marriage, and worried whether the married life of Catholics was being eroded by so much divorce in our time. I can remember gatherings of divorced Catholics where bishops came to speak, but their nervousness left them sounding somewhat distant and remote, repeating warnings about the Church's teaching and discipline. Today their heartfelt compassion is coming through much more clearly. In recent years bishops have translated their concern about married life into many vital new programs to help Catholics marry better and stay married. This period, which has witnessed the development of the Church's ministry to divorced Catholics, has also witnessed a rebirth of the family life movement and increasingly effective programs in the Church community to prevent divorce.

Our bishops, good shepherds that they are, seem to be learning that, whatever the risks may be, they must be present to their people when they suffer and must bring to them the strong, confident, healing words of Christ. At another Florida conference, the year before, Archbishop Edward McCarthy of Miami, welcomed several hundred divorced men and women: "You are very important to the Catholic community. Where once you witnessed the love and fidelity of Christ to the world in your married life together, now as divorced persons you witness to the cross of Christ. You tell the world that the suffering of divorce is not the end of love, but rather the beginning of new life in Christ."

Numerous bishops across the two countries have now written pastoral letters to their people on marriage and divorce; others have gone on television to invite back separated, divorced and divorced/remarried persons who have become disaffected from the Church; many have given precious budgetary support to full-time Church workers in this area. Divorce ministry is becoming more and more a collaborative ministry—bishops, priests, sisters, laity, all working together.

Not that all the bishops have provided the leadership on this issue we would like. I remember talking to a woman in one diocese where the bishop had not been supportive of efforts to help the divorced. I thought she might be angry at the bishop, but she said, "We pray for the bishop every day. We know God will open his heart and help him understand us." I think she put her finger on the most important strategy for effective change in the Church. It is prayerful, loving people, witnessing in a Christian manner about their concerns, who move mountains. I encourage lay people to ask to see their bishops, to help him get to know them, and to help him understand the nature of this ministry.

At a regional divorce conference in Omaha in the spring of 1983, Bishop Anthony Milone challenged the people present to pray for and minister to their bishops and priests. He admitted that he had misunderstood this ministry for a long time and had even been somewhat afraid of divorced people. But then he got involved in a parish discussion group over some months with divorced people, and his eyes were opened. He had come to appreciate the sincerity, courage and faith of his divorced parishioners, and was deeply impressed by the concrete ways they were reaching out to help each other and help the whole parish. He ended his homily with a plea, "We bishops need you very much."

Pope John Paul II

I was helping with the divorced Catholics group at Holy Trinity Church in Washington, D.C. when Pope John Paul II made his pastoral visit to the United States in 1979. The final Mass of his visit was held on the Washington Mall, and had as its theme, "Respect Life." Representatives of all the Catholic family life organizations were invited to sit prominently near the altar, including Roni Bissett of Seattle, then chairperson of the Board of the North American Conference of Separated and Divorced Catholics. The previous Tuesday I had encouraged the people at the Holy Trinity group to come to the Papal Mass; there were men and women from several other divorced Catholics groups present, and one carried a popular sign, "God loves divorced Catholics."

The morning after the Pope's Mass I received a call from a member of the group at Holy Trinity. "I just want you to know that I walked out at the end of his homily. I felt insulted. All he talked about was the permanence of marriage, and the evils of contraception, abortion and divorce. I couldn't find one word of encouragement for us."

I told her that I had listened closely to what the Pope had said, and had a different reaction. I didn't object to anything he said about divorce, but I felt it was unfortunate that some other positive things about divorced Catholics were not said. We chatted on the phone for a good while. "Don't even the divorced regret their divorces?" I asked. The divorced, we both agreed, most of all wish that there was no divorce in the world. The divorced most of all know the value of a permanent marriage, wish they had not gotten a divorce, and certainly don't want their children to get divorced. I think we are all one with the Pope in standing for lasting marriages and against divorce. That is the teaching of Jesus in Scripture, and for two thousand years the Church has stood for lasting marriage and against divorce. I fully expected the Pope to take that position, and I think it is important for us all in the Church community that he does so loudly and clearly.

Yet, I continued, we know that many marriages are tragic and destructive, and that many sincere Christian men and women need to divorce. Divorce can be a very Christian solution to a very bad situation, and it can enable people to salvage broken lives. We know that the same Lord who stood for permanence and against divorce also reached out with real tenderness and understanding to the divorced in his own day. I said I wished that the Pope could have included some words of sympathy for those who experience the heartbreak of broken marriage. Maybe, I suggested, much of the awareness that we've developed in this country in helping divorced persons is somewhat foreign to this new Pope. We Americans do have the highest divorce rate in the world, and we've had the most divorce for the longest time of any of the world's nations. I would hope that in time we could familiarize the Pope with the insights we've gained which enable us to balance permanence and compassion, and not see compassion to the divorced as something which threatens the Church's teaching on the permanence of marriage. My own experience is that our compassion toward the divorced makes the Church's overall teaching on marriage more attractive to our world. We are beginning to show that we are believing men and women who can take some very strong stands—against violence, for permanence in marriage, for the poor of the world; yet we can be most understanding of those who fail at these commitments and struggle to rebuild their lives.

In the years since, Pope John Paul II has become a more universal shepherd through his extensive travels, and has been influenced by the Christian people he has met around the world. In this time he has made several of the most important statements ever made by a Pope about divorce. In 1980 he welcomed to Rome over two hundred bishops from around the world to advise him about the problems faced by Christian families in our world today, and divorce was one of the problems that received serious attention. Archbishop Derek Warlock, speaking for the bishops of Great Britain, eloquently laid out the case for Church ministry to the divorced; bishops from other nations, including the United States, verbalized their concern. The Pope took all of the bishops' speeches under consideration, and a year later responded with a letter to Catholics throughout the world, in which he said: "I earnestly call upon pastors and the whole community of the faithful to help the divorced and with solicitous care to make sure that they do not consider themselves as separated from the Church, for as baptized persons they can and indeed must share in her life. They should be encouraged to listen to the word of God, to attend the Sacrifice of the Mass, to persevere in prayer, to contribute to works of charity and to community efforts in favor of justice, to bring up their children in the Christian faith, to cultivate the spirit and practice of penance, and thus implore, day by day, God's grace. Let the Church pray for them, encourage them and show herself a merciful mother and thus sustain them in faith and hope . . . ."

First of all the Pope makes it clear that divorce or remarriage does not separate one from the Church. There is no excommunication in universal Church law or in local church law which separates a divorced or remarried Catholic from the Church. (There was an unfortunate excommunication attached to a second marriage "outside the Church" in the United States, but it was removed by Pope Paul VI in 1977 at the request of the American bishops.) This means that the divorced and even the divorced/remarried remain part of the communion of saints and share in the blessings which come to those who are part of our family of faith.

All too often the divorced and the divorced/remarried have been treated with contempt and denied pastoral care. Here we find John Paul II encouraging them to participate in the life of the Church, to pray, work for justice and lead exemplary lives. He has obviously been touched himself by many good divorced and divorced/remarried persons, and offers an approving evaluation of their Christian lives. Nowhere does he call the divorced and remarried sinners. He then calls upon the whole Church community to encourage them and sustain them. How often have divorced and remarried persons felt ostracized by family or "good Catholics." The Holy Father challenges all those attitudes and dispositions which would condemn and judge the divorced and remarried.

When the Pope was in Washington, D.C. he visited a group of handicapped children and adults on the lawn of Trinity College. Some bystanders have reported that as he was moving along the people, a crippled, blind child called out, "Holy Father, bless me!" The Pope knelt down before her wheelchair and blessed her, caressing the child. As he leaned close to her, he whispered, "Bless me!"

The same tenderness the Pope showed these handicapped persons, he extends to all suffering people, including the divorced. On his pastoral visit to England in 1982, he preached: "We must reach out with love—the love of Christ to those who know the pain of failure in marriage, to those who know the loneliness of bringing up a family on their own; to those whose family life is dominated by tragedy or illness of mind or body. I praise all those who help people wounded by the breakdown of their marriage by showing them Christ's compassion and counseling them according to Christ's truths."

Pope John Paul II incorporates in his public speeches the same wonderful balance we find in the teaching of Jesus. Just as the Lord called his followers to commit themselves to each other in marriages that last until death and yet reached out with warmth and acceptance to those who had divorced, so the Pope is stressing in his ministry for the whole Church the same balance between permanence and compassion.

Annulments

"*I* can't get an annulment, Father. I can't say I wasn't ever married. I have the scars to prove it!" I've heard statements like that so often.

There is a tremendous amount of misunderstanding that surrounds annulments in the Catholic Church today. Some people say they will never get an annulment because they will never make their children illegitimate. Others insist that you have to be rich or well-connected to get one. Persistent reports claim that annulments cost thousands of dollars. Some just don't feel they could ever face their spouse again and drag up all that painful business; they're getting along now, and don't want to ruin the fragile peace they've achieved.

In order to understand what an annulment is, one has to understand what the Catholic Church teaches a good marriage is. Many times in talking with groups I ask the people to list for me some of the qualities that they feel are necessary for a good, contemporary marriage. They list things such as "fidelity," "sense of humor," "commitment," "compatibility," "love," "honesty," "sacrifice," "generosity," "forgiveness," "good sexual adjustment," and on and on. The Church feels that a Christian marriage involves all those things too. The Church begins its definition of a good marriage with the same fundamental human qualities that we people living in the last quarter of the twentieth century in the Western industrial nations consider as making a good marriage. A Christian marriage is a human reality

201

which becomes through faith something much more—a sign of God's love in the world. We Americans arrived at a society-wide consensus that marriage involves a loving commitment between two people who give themselves joyfully and happily to each other for life.

The bishops of the world, meeting at the Second Vatican Council in 1965, defined marriage for us today by saying that it is fundamentally the establishment of a "community of life and love" between husband and wife. That relationship necessarily involves a commitment until death, and is a life-giving commitment. Both give life to each other, give life to their children, and give life to all who are touched by their love. Their faith helps them see deeper significance in their relationship; they see the love of God for all people breaking into history in their love for each other. Christian marriage is the best human approximation we can come to of the tender love of God for all humankind.

I then asked the divorced to think whether their marriage reached that level of development. Did such a fundamental relationship of loving commitment, happiness, and personal well-being come to exist between them? Many will admit sadly that their marriages never came close to that standard. An annulment is a decision by the Church that even though two people were married in church and lived together as husband and wife and even had children, no relationship ever came to exist between them which could be called a "community of life and love." That's not to say that they didn't enter marriage sincerely and didn't give it a real try. Many may have persisted in bad times and sought advice and counseling; they didn't take to the thought of divorce easily and resisted the suggestion for a long time. But gradually they came to realize that nothing was happening between them—they were not growing closer; in fact, they were growing increasingly apart. They were not thriving in this relationship; rather there were signs of personal deterioration all around. The decision to divorce was a painful admission that the situation was hopeless.

Sometimes such marriages come about because people are simply mismatched. He might well be able to build a happy marriage with someone else, or she might be able to find happiness with another person. An annulment is a decision that these two people did not have the necessary personal resources to build a lasting marriage relationship with each other. We see many individuals today, after an annulment, making a successful second marriage to a different person.

There are many other marriages that seem doomed from the start. One or both parties may have some emotional disability, such as ongoing depression, inability to settle down and hold a job, serious alcoholism, or the after-effects of trauma in war. There are many seriously wounded persons in our society, whose wounds seem to be inflamed by the tensions and demands of married life. Some people fare well as single people, but, once married, they come apart. Sometimes even homosexuals marry, and only later discover that they are not suited for marriage.

The Catholic Church takes marriage commitments very seriously. When couples marry in church we hold them to their vows and try to support them in building a lasting marriage until death. Yet the Church does not hold people to vows they were unable to make, or vows that were doomed from the start because one or both parties were unable to be married for life. An annulment is a merciful way the Church frees people from marriage promises that were impossible for them to keep.

Catholic audiences never fail me when I ask them the definition of a sacrament. Everyone learned that a sacrament is an outward sign, instituted by Christ, to give grace. "What's the outward sign in marriage?" I like to ask. Some will answer the ring, others the ceremony, but few give the real answer. The sign in the sacrament of matrimony is the couple themselves. It's the couple who are the something seen, which points to something unseen. Just as in Holy Communion, the bread and the wine are seen and point to the presence of Christ who is unseen; so in matrimony the husband and wife in their love for one another point to the love of God which is not seen. For marriage to be a sacrament there has to be a strong, loving, committed relationship between husband and wife, one that has the potential to endure until death. The Church isn't saying that a sacramental marriage is nothing but happiness and good times; every marriage is tested and its love deepened by sacrifice and hard times, and every lasting relationship involves reaching deeper through times of stress and strain. An annulment is a decision by the Church that a particular marriage was never a sacramental union. The relationship between this man and woman never reached that level of loving commitment which would make it a sign of God's loving commitment to us all. The Church is saying that if we struggle to find some human reality which can help us understand how much God loves us, there may be no better reality available to us than to look at the devoted, loving relationship of a Christian man and wife. Because the Church takes marriage so seriously and believes that the strength of Catholic marriages is so important to the Church community, it does not hold people to marriages that show no such sign of human love and commitment.

In order to get an annulment, the Church suggests that one party contact a parish priest and initiate the process at the parish level. The local priest sends the completed information along to the Church office which handles the cases, called the marriage tribunal. An annulment is a public decision by the Church, and it is recorded in the public records of the Church. Therefore the Church needs to get a good picture of the story of this marriage, what happened from the beginning to the end, so that it can make a good decision about its possible annulment. The priest gathers basic information about the marriage, and usually asks the particular spouse, who is beginning the case, to write out in his or her own words the story of the marriage with all significant details. The person who initiates the case is asked to suggest several witnesses, family or close friends, who can fill in the details of the case and back up the assertions made by this spouse. Since an annulment is a decision about a marriage which involved two persons, the Church always contacts the other party and invites him or her to participate in the process. The parties are not asked to argue in front of one another or prove one another wrong. Even when both participate, their testimony is taken separately and is kept confidential. The Church has no desire to put further strain on the relationship. When the other person cooperates, the completion of the case is made much easier. Yet if the other person refuses to participate, this does not stop the process. The Church usually can get the necessary information from other suggested resources, keeping the non-cooperative party informed of any decision made.

This beginning process of gathering information, writing the history of the marriage, and contacting witnesses may take about six to nine months, sometimes shorter, sometimes longer. When the priest in charge of the case is satisfied that he has all the necessary information, he presents the case to a panel of three judges, who make the final decision. The judges meet by themselves. There is no Perry Mason-style courtroom in which the former husband and wife are asked to testify before each other and their friends.

In the United States, most annulment cases are processed in about a year. The Church usually requests a contribution to help defray the costs of the process; in the United States the average cost is $250. Some dioceses ask for nothing; in all others, if the individuals cannot afford a contribution, the fee is waived.

Many people have told me that they found the annulment process a healing experience. They felt unburdened by writing their marriage history, as difficult as it was at first. When the

annulment was granted they wept tears of joy, feeling released
from the disastrous marriage. Others have told me that the piece
of paper from the diocesan tribunal was a symbol that the
Church cared and the Church understood. "I had the feeling
that the Church was telling me that this marriage had been a
mistake, and that I did the right thing in getting a divorce," one
young woman told me. An annulment is not a decision that two
people were never married; rather, it is a decision by the Church
that their marriage had never developed into that kind of solid
human relationship, that "community of life and love," which
we call a sacrament.

Furthermore it should be noted that children are not made
illegitimate by an annulment of their parents' marriage. Legitimacy is first of all a civil concern; this marriage was registered
civilly at the time it was celebrated in church, so it has both a
civil and a religious character. The civil aspects of the marriage
are resolved by the civil divorce, the religious aspects by the
Church annulment. The children's legitimacy is guaranteed by
the civil nature of the marriage even though it has ended in divorce; the Church annulment does not penalize the children in
any way in their continuing life as Christians. Thus the children are not affected civilly or religiously by the annulment of
their parents' marriage.

The men and women of the Church's marriage tribunals
remain some of the most important servants in the Church's
overall compassionate ministry to the divorced and remarried.

Justice

Often people ask me what the greatest single cause of divorce is in the United States today. I answer quite readily, "Poverty." That surprises people who expect me to say lack of communication, changing male/female roles, alcoholism, or collapse of traditional values. The poor have always had the most divorce, although much of it has always gone unnoticed in the larger society. We know that it's getting no easier today for economically deprived people in the United States. The poor marry at the youngest ages because there is no good reason to postpone marriage, since they usually do not go to college or take a job which requires several years of travel and round-the-clock investment. The younger couples are when they marry, the more children they have; young children create more financial stress and usually push the young mother out to find some kind of temporary work just to make ends meet. Take a young couple who are of average maturity for their age, burden them with child-rearing in an atmosphere of financial strain, put them in a community which does not have good community resources and may not be a very safe place to live, and you can begin to see the multiple pressures on the marriages of the poor.

Over the last generation we have begun to count more of the divorces of the poor. Community legal services and public assistance made such legal resolution of failed relationships necessary.

Seventy-five years ago, observers pointed to "poor man's divorce," by which they meant desertion, because in those days many poor people who did not succeed at marriage simply took off and later lived in a common law relationship with another person. Some may have been "married" several times without ever formalizing such arrangements and without ever having them recorded in civil records.

Often when we think about the poor we think immediately of poor black people, but in the United States the majority of the poor are white people living in the cities or in rural areas. The growing population of the poor in many of our states today includes many people of Hispanic origin. Given all the social and economic changes that have affected most of our society over recent generations, there remains at the bottom of the heap an almost immovable population of poor people whose pervasive problems include a large amount of family disintegration and divorce.

We have always liked to believe in the United States that hard times bring families closer together. There is some truth in that for some people. One sociologist, Robert S. Weiss, suggests that during hard times when some couples feel threatened by the possibility of losing a job and possibly losing house and car and all they've built up over a lifetime, they become more tolerant of each other's faults and less likely to want to part because of dissatisfaction with each other. Yet for many others prolonged unemployment can be the extra burden which pushes a fragile marriage over the brink. In 1982 unemployment reached one American household in three, according to a N.Y. Times/CBS poll. Rob McDonald says that he started drinking after he lost his job as a real estate salesman; his wife and children left him for six months. "I blamed myself and drowned myself in booze," he said. Fortunately after alcoholism treatment he was able to get a new job and save his marriage. Lillian Morris lost her job as head checker in a supermarket when it went out of business. "I had a car—I lost that. I had my own home—I had to move back with my mother. Soon after my husband and I were so worn down by financial wrangling, we separated."

Forty-seven percent of the unemployed in the study reported more family arguments and marital tension. The anxieties rising from the unemployment problem seem to produce a generalized depressing effect on the quality of family life. Men who have been raised to see their dignity involved in being a provider for their wives and families feel a loss of manhood when out of work for an extended period. When a wife has to take on marginal work to keep the family going, such role reversals create great strain. Men may pitch in with the housework while a wife is away, but they usually don't like it. A researcher at Johns Hopkins University found the association of family conflict with prolonged unemployment of critical importance since many jobs are expected to be permanently lost in the recent recession. Researchers have found, in addition to an upsurge in couples looking for marriage counseling and divorcing, evidence of extreme violence and aggressive behavior, and even higher suicide levels. A union shop steward in southern Illinois recently reported just such tragic events affecting his unemployed members in record numbers.

Separated and divorced persons have long known discrimination in hiring and finding housing. One woman told me that she had a most difficult time finding a smaller house after her divorce, until she decided to present herself as a widow, and then real estate agents treated her differently. The *Wall Street Journal* reported recently that many firms have found divorced men and women highly motivated and hard-working employees. "Maybe it's because this job means so much to them that they try so hard," one employer observed. Yet the widespread impression that divorced people have not proved competent in handling their personal lives and must be flawed individuals still haunts many divorced people looking for work. For divorced women, forced to re-enter the work force to support a family, it often becomes a succession of marginal jobs that are offered because of her "unique circumstances." The fact that only 40% of American women are still receiving custody payments for children a year after the final divorce decree points up the stressful economic circumstances of so many single parents.

Through its support groups and all the other aspects of divorce ministry the Church is reaching out to help divorcing people. Within these groups, much practical charity has flourished where groups rally around financially-strapped individuals and provide emergency and short-term assistance. Helpful new friends from divorce groups can provide good leads on jobs and direct people to good legal counsel which can help them get available public aid. Some divorce groups have developed their own outreach programs to other hurting people in the parish such as the blind, the handicapped and the elderly, or have joined in other parish-wide efforts to help the less fortunate.

Yet many group members are learning that charity is not enough. The external stresses which tear apart so many fragile marriage relationships—unemployment, poverty, racism—are rooted in the economic and social structures of the society and require political and social action to bring about change. "Action on behalf of justice is constitutive of the preaching of the Gospel," some 200 bishops from all over the world wrote at the end of the 1971 Roman synod on Justice in the World. There is a growing consciousness in the Catholic community that Christians must band together and unite themselves with all men and women of conscience and integrity to help build a better society in which ordinary people can have a chance to build the happy married lives they want. Many divorced Catholics are participating in parish based programs such as RENEW which seek to raise awareness about the long tradition of Catholic social teaching and its necessary application to our own time.

A coalition of black leaders recently issued *A Policy Framework for Racial Justice* in which they pointed to the unique problems afflicting the black family in the United States. They noted that 48% of black families with children under age 18 are headed by women, that more than half of the black babies born in America are born out of wedlock, and that black families are beset disproportionately with divorce and separation and by racism and other destabilizing forces. The leaders observe that programs ostensibly designed to assist low-income blacks and other poor Americans have had the perverse effect of locking them into poverty by cutting off the bottom rungs of the ladder of economic progress. They call for a national full-employment program, a major overhaul of public assistance with emphasis on work incentives, and other new government policies to help black families move toward stability and self-reliance. All of us in the Church's ministry to the divorced admit that we have not been as successful in reaching out to help poor people as we would like. We rejoice in the existence of some predominantly black and Hispanic groups in our cities and some groups which are reaching out to the rural poor. We know that such direct action must be coupled with larger Church action at the local and national level to bring about the necessary changes in social policy which will help poor families.

There are also many justice issues in American society which affect the divorced woman, including support enforcement, day care for working mothers, pension reform, establishment of personal credit after divorce, and tax relief for female heads of households. There are also difficult justice issues affecting older divorced women who can be reduced to poverty by a divorce late in life.

The tragic legacy of the Vietnam war continues to be felt in the community of the divorced. Many tribunals grant annulments today because of "post-Vietnam syndrome" which refers to that mix of violent behavior and fear of intimacy which many veterans of that war carry like a battle scar. The Veterans Administration says that there are some 300,000 Vietnam vets who have been left emotionally disabled by the war. I have known some of these vets and their former wives who have become active in the Catholic peace movement as an attempt to prevent future wars and even the talk of war. Pope John XXIII in his great encyclical *Pacem in Terris* said that peace was not just the absence of armed conflict among people, but more the presence of positive relationships among people, between governments and within the whole world community. Divorced people are men and women who know something about positive and negative relationships, and many of them today are translating that learning into action for peace and justice. Many support group meetings or divorced Catholics liturgies end with the familiar song, "Let there be peace on earth, and let it begin with me."

If the suffering of divorce becomes a school in which men and women grow to new awareness of the causes of the suffering around them and begin to act, all in their own way and in their own place, for social change and justice, then the suffering of divorce will not have been wasted. As overwhelming as the roots of injustice may seem, the Lord calls us to believe that one person of vision and action can make a difference. Robert Kennedy in 1968 told the students of South Africa that every time a man or woman stands up for justice, his or her action sends forth a tiny ripple of hope, and that ripple of hope, united with similar ripples all over the world, can tear down the mightiest walls of oppression and injustice.

Evalgelization

Over the last several years, more and more people who are not Roman Catholics have been coming to Catholic support groups. Some come with Catholic friends; others come because there is no other help available for divorcing people in their area; still others say they are attracted by the religious character of the groups, and have been looking for something more than just social opportunities for the separated and divorced. In some places the presence of so many non-Catholics has created uneasiness among Catholic leaders, fearful of a loss of Catholic identity and Catholic spiritual distinctiveness. Many of those who come belong to Protestant churches and some are devout Jews, but most are people who have belonged to no church during their adult life. I like to insist that these "strangers" are presenting a marvelous opportunity for divorce groups, and these newcomers may well have been led here by the Spirit.

It is estimated that there are 80 million Americans who belong to no church. They are not necessarily people who do not believe in God, but their lives have not been marked by church membership; yet they experience the trauma of divorce as a "spiritual crisis." Divorce for them raises the same questions about the ultimate meaning of life, personal values and personal goals. It's easy to understand why such people are drawn to Catholic support groups. One such man I met at a workshop in New Mexico told me, "I really felt lost after my divorce. I was spiritually at sea, until a friend invited me to this group, and I found what I had been looking for."

Cardinal Lavigerie, the founder of the White Fathers of Africa, when asked what evangelization was, replied, "We go among the people and perform the corporal works of mercy—opening schools, hospitals, shelters. When they ask us why we do it, we tell them about Jesus Christ." Support groups should welcome anyone who comes in need of comfort, support and healing. Let them relate as they are able, participate as they feel comfortable. In time they will hear members speak of Jesus of Nazareth and their faith in him and how it has transformed their suffering and given them new hope. That's evangelization.

Jesus said, "Whoever welcomes the least of my brothers and sisters welcomes me." Hospitality may be the most distinguishing characteristic of a genuine Christian community. I like to insist that welcoming the stranger may be the most important test of the Christian spirit of a group—not just welcoming the person who is unknown, but also welcoming the "strange" person. We know there are so many people who suffer serious emotional effects of a broken marriage; they may be chronically depressed, not take very good care of themselves, and be wearying in their often inappropriate behavior. Others go through short periods of serious upset. The capacity to welcome people such as these is at the heart of the Gospel. I have seen such "strange" people helped enormously by the warm acceptance of a divorce group, and have seen their behavior begin to improve significantly. The healing that the group offers may well be to rescue such men and women from a downward emotional spiral.

Pope Paul VI said that the Church's mission of evangelization has a twofold thrust: first to the unchurched, and, second, to alienated Catholics. And he insisted that the two are closely linked. The Church's reconciling ministry to Catholics who have become alienated from the Church over divorce and remarriage has become today an effective tool of evangelization. Certainly a Church that ministers to its hurting members and offers them hope and community is a Church that will be attractive to those who feel lost after marital breakdown. Divorced Catholics as they reach out to welcome and heal hurting divorced people, Catholic or not, are becoming instruments of evangelization. By living the Gospel message of love and acceptance and by witnessing it to a suffering world, they make the Gospel attractive and contemporary.

In many places across the United States and Canada not only have divorced Catholics been welcomed home because of divorce ministry, but many unchurched divorced people have sought membership in the Catholic community. A priest friend in California who prepares people for reception into the Catholic Church says that the divorced people in his program seem to understand the meaning of Christianity best. "They know very well the meaning of Christ's love, fidelity, rejection, death and resurrection, because they've been through it themselves. Becoming a Catholic is for many of them an experience of coming home—of finding a community which offers a way of understanding and celebrating the ways God has already touched their lives."

The Church's mission of evangelization—making Christ known to the world—is often hampered by the divisions among Christians. Jesus prayed that "all may be one . . . so that the world may believe that you have sent me." The unity of Christians should be an effect of faith in Christ, and disunity among Christians is a scandal, weakening the witness of the Gospel, and often seeming to compromise the good that Christians do. The last four Popes have made Christian unity their number one priority, and Pope John Paul II says that he prays for unity every day.

Divorce hurts the same whether one is a Methodist, an Episcopalian, or a Roman Catholic. A growing cooperation across the continent among the churches in ministering to the divorced is one of the most impressive developments I've seen in recent years. Divorced men and women of all faiths are becoming instruments in building up the unity of the Church. This movement among divorced people is truly a work of the Spirit, and it will contribute to the unity of the Church, since the Spirit is a Spirit of unity and peace.

In some places local ecumenical church groups have developed a common support ministry for the separated and divorced. In other places where Protestant and Catholic churches have their own individual support groups, they get together from time to time for common programs and social events. Catholics are not the only ones who have known neglect and even ostracization in their local church communities. Many divorced Protestants complain of similar problems in their own churches, underscoring the observation that the rejection and harsh disapproval of the divorced is a very American problem. Divorced Catholics, Episcopalians and Protestants working together are becoming a source of pastoral renewal for all their churches, as all seek to make the divorced welcome and as all reach out to those who have become alienated.

This ground of ecumenical cooperation often is a new footing for many Catholics. I like to offer these ecumenical pioneers the following advice. First of all, don't be afraid to be Catholic, yet avoid positions of religious superiority. We Catholics have our strengths and weaknesses as do Episcopalians and Protestants. It should be noted that it is inappropriate for Catholics to try to "convert" church-going Episcopalians and Protestants. We need to work side by side in renewing our own churches. One Lutheran pastor observed that Catholics have probably done a better job over the years in affirming the Lord's call to permanence in marriage, while many Protestants have probably done a better job in affirming the Lord's call to compassion for the divorced. We need each other, he suggested, to find the appropriate Gospel balance. Second, Catholics can tend to be "heady" at times, since we have such a long intellectual tradition, and we sometimes need help in being more affectively supportive. But it's important for us not to lose our heads and go only with our hearts when dealing with these complex issues. There's a Catholic instinct toward thinking things through which can be a great help to hurting people, while there is a Protestant quality of easy acceptance which we could well imitate.

Third, there is a great renewal in everyday spirituality for lay people going on in all the churches. Sharing resources for prayer and Christian living can be most enriching. Catholics and Protestants have had somewhat different styles of community which seems to be evidenced by the fact that Catholics form groups so easily, while Protestants often seem more personally self-assertive. One Episcopal minister told me that the greatest gift he felt Catholics brought to an ecumenical support group was their informality. "You Catholics can be authoritarian, but we Episcopalians can be awfully reserved," he confessed.

Being instruments of evangelization and ecumenism doesn't mean that people in support groups have to take on a weighty new agenda. It means, for me, continuing to do what they do so well. Being welcoming, caring, open to all—these fundamental Christian dispositions are the very qualities that preach the Gospel and contribute to the healing of the Church's divisions. Those who work for unity in all the Churches say that we don't know the ultimate design and form that God has in mind for his Church; all we do know is that the forms that have kept us apart will have to change, and the shape of the Christian people in the future may be beyond our most imaginative projections. Likewise, the struggle of the Church to free itself from its own self-absorption and internal needs and begin to focus on the larger needs of humanity to which it is sent—that struggle is part of the process of evangelization and is beginning to purify the Church and prepare it for great works to come.

It is said that one is either part of the solution or part of the problem of Church unity and evangelization. I like to feel that separated, divorced and remarried Catholics, ministering to one another and reaching out to minister with other Christians, are contributing both to the preaching of the Gospel in our time and the eventual unity of the Church. It may seem odd to think that the divorced would become instruments of evangelization and ecumenism, but hasn't the Lord in every age raised up the most unlikely persons to be the instruments of his peace?

Holiness

"Can recovery from divorce be a pathway to holiness?" I asked a group in Michigan. Louise spoke up energetically: "Sure, I want to get my life together again, and sure I want to live as a good Christian, but holiness? That's not for me. I've got kids to raise, and a job, and a lot of faults which just don't seem to go away. I've never been a holy roller or one of those people who seem to live up in the clouds. Sure, I've known some saints in my life, but I never thought of myself in those terms."

Holiness, I told the group, summons up images for most of us like Louise's wonderful description. Holiness is something for those rare birds who are a little different, people who go to church and prayer meetings all the time. Nothing could be farther from the truth. Let me begin by proposing that holiness is wholeness. It means that holiness, being God-like, comes when one is humanly whole. For divorced people struggling to recover from a broken marriage, it means that they are on a two-track process: the first track, the whole very human process of reshaping one's life, developing new resources, and learning to love again; and then a second track, which is the whole attempt to be a good Christian amid the tensions and opportunities of this new life situation. Holiness, as we understand it today in the Church, means that both tracks are really the same track. The whole very human process of building a new life after divorce is for the believing person itself the way to holiness. Being a good Christian means being first of all a good human being. Having one's life truly together here on earth suggests that one's life is together with God. Learning to be tolerant, accepting and forgiving in one's life after divorce is a way of becoming more like God. What God cares about in our lives is not just how many hours we spend in church and how many cans we collect for the Thanksgiving drive—as important as those things may be. What he cares about is the way we are getting our lives together as human beings. The more we root bitterness, hostility and fear out of our lives, the closer we come to other people, and the closer we come to God. Support groups and counseling may be as important for us in this process as prayer groups and spiritual direction.

I remember meeting a woman once who told me that she had put all the pain of divorce in God's hands, and she had found peace. I was aware of the woman's personal life and of the fact that it was not going well. I knew she had serious financial problems with a husband who was not giving her support, and she was doing nothing about it; I knew her kids were acting in strange ways, but she was looking the other way; I knew that underneath this pious, calm exterior she was seething with anger and resentment but she was unable to face it. I told her that I was sure God had taken her under his care and loved her very much, but I also told her that here on earth God's work must be our own. Here on earth God expects us to roll up our sleeves and take responsibility for our lives. He trusts us to marshal our resources and do something about our problems. Sure, he is always with us, strengthening and helping us, but sometimes his strength and help may take the form of a kick in the pants. I told her that I thought it was highly unlikely that God was going to show up in the flesh and settle these financial arrangements, get her kids under control, or erase her own bitter feelings. Some of the people in the group had told me that they were completely frustrated in trying to reach her because she had developed this holy glaze which seemed to protect her from all unwelcome intrusions. She resisted me at first, but after several conversations and a worsening of the situation, she began to take some initiative and straighten out the turmoil in her life. Gradually, with the help of a high school adjustment counselor, a very kind parish lawyer, and some very faithful divorced friends, she began to experience some success in dealing with her problems. In the process she seemed to become less "holy," less demonstrative in talking about God, and she even missed a few prayer meetings, but I think she began to move more surely toward genuine Christian holiness.

Different people have different religious styles. Some people talk freely about God and like to share their conversations with him, while others have a hard time many days believing there is a God at all. Some take to quiet prayer and solitude like fish to water, while others have a hard time remembering morning and evening prayers. Some people have incredibly beautiful experiences of God's love and presence, the kind that make you tingle a little when they talk about them, while others seem to experience most powerfully the absence of God. God is present to us as the people we are; he touches different lives in different ways, yet he touches each life. He calls us all to himself, and he calls us as we are. It is foolish to compare religious experiences or to try to measure the depth of one person's faith life against another. Spiritual superiority or elitism seems to suggest somewhat arrogantly that we know for certain the exact style of God's presence in each of our lives. He gives out many different gifts, St. Paul warns us, to many different people in many different ways for many different reasons. What's most important is never to think that certain signs mean that this person is closer to God than another. Remember that in the Gospel Jesus said it was the publican who beat his breast at the back of the temple and who said, "God, have mercy on me a sinner," who went home justified.

All the ways divorced Catholics reach out to shake and help

and urge each other along to build new lives and become new people—all this is the pathway to holiness. Good friends who reach out to sustain and care for each other and help people through the worst are the best spiritual guides. Priests and religious are important partners to this process of spiritual healing and recovery, teaching, praying with the group, and celebrating the sacraments, but those special ministries of word and sacrament are most effective when they build on solid soil prepared by the hard work of human recovery. God invites us all to place ourselves and our anxieties in his hands, but he also gives us the necessary energy to do something about those things. He doesn't usually provide overnight miracles; he respects us too much for that. He reverences the slow but sure ways we grow and change and recover, and he is with us all throughout that process. He is with us to bear us up at the lowest points and fill our hearts with joy at the highest points. There is a true but very mysterious way in which he is our partner in recovery, all the while working through our own decisions and our own gritty courage in ways that enable us to feel that our recovery has been truly our own, in our own way, in our own time. In the recovery process God helps us draw out of the tortured, growing, changing people we are, our best selves—our holiest selves.

Several years ago a reporter spent three days covering one of our national conferences at the University of Notre Dame. When it was all over she told me that one of the most significant things she had noticed was the quality of the singing at our final liturgy. I was puzzled by what she meant. "I covered the national conference of the charismatics here several weeks ago, but their singing was very different. They sang like birds—there was something incredibly musical, almost other-worldly about their singing. The divorced Catholics' singing was different—it was throatier, not quite as harmonious. It said something to me about two different spiritualities—the charismatics' is more other-worldly, the divorced Catholics' is more down to earth."

The spirituality, the holiness, that we see emerging among separated, divorced and remarried Catholics in the United States is just as the reporter said—a spirituality, a holiness born of suffering, rejection and pain, rooted in the real struggles of everyday life, yet reaching to God and finding him in coming to new life through that very suffering and in those very struggles. Spirituality and holiness in the Christian community takes on many authentic shapes and styles, but the earthy style of the divorced is one the Church needs today very much.

Works Cited and Other Important Sources

Bane, Mary Jo. *Here To Stay: American Families in the Twentieth Century*. New York: Basic Books, 1976.

Cleveland, Martha. "Divorce in the Middle Years: The Sexual Dimension," *Journal of Divorce* 2 (1979): 255–262.

Kelly, Kevin T. *Divorce and Second Marriage*. New York: Seabury, 1983.

Krantzler, Mel. *Creative Divorce*. New York: M. Evans and Co., 1973.

Levinson, Daniel. *The Seasons of a Man's Life*. New York: Knopf, 1978.

McBrien, Richard. *Catholicism*. Minneapolis: Winston, 1980.

McNeill, Donald P., Morrison, Douglas A., and Nouwen, Henri J.M. *Compassion*. New York: Doubleday, 1982.

Nouwen, Henri J.M. *Clowning in Rome*. New York: Doubleday Image Books, 1979.

―――. *The Wounded Healer*. New York: Doubleday Image Books, 1979.

O'Brien, Judith and Gene O'Brien. *A Redeeming State: A Handbook for Couples Planning Remarriage in the Church*. New York: Paulist Press, 1983.

Ripple, Paula. *Called To Be Friends*. Notre Dame, Indiana: Ave Maria Press, 1980.

————. *The Pain and the Possibility*. Notre Dame, Indiana: Ave Maria Press, 1978.

————. *Walking with Loneliness*. Notre Dame, Indiana: Ave Maria Press, 1982.

Weiss, Robert S. *Going It Alone*. New York: Basic Books, 1979.

————. *Loneliness*. Cambridge, Massachusetts: MIT Press, 1974.

————. *Marital Separation*. New York: Basic Books, 1979.

Whitehead, Evelyn E. and James D. *Christian Life Patterns*. New York: Doubleday, 1979.

————. *Marrying Well*. New York: Doubleday, 1981.

Young, James J. *Growing Through Divorce*. New York: Paulist Press, 1979.

————. *When You're Divorced and Catholic*. St. Meinrad, Indiana: Abbey Press, 1980.

Young, James J., ed. *Divorce Ministry and the Marriage Tribunal*. New York: Paulist Press, 1982.

————. *Ministering to the Divorced Catholic*. New York: Paulist Press, 1979.